Power UP!

Emotional Relearning™
Through Scriptures

FIRST EDITION

Ronald E. Ovitt

GILGAL PUBLISHING
12540 S. 68th Ct.
Palos Heights, IL 60463

POWER UP!

Power Up!

©2018 by Ronald E. Ovitt
Gilgal Publishing, Inc.
12540 68th Ct.
Palos Heights, IL 60463
www.empowerministry.org
Printed in the United States of America

Other Gilgal books by Ronald E. Ovitt

- Wired For Ministry: Activate Passions, Experiences & Abilities
- Moment in The Word: Daily Moments That Feed Your Soul
- The Five Signs of a Healthy Christian: How to Be a Spiritually Vibrant and Healthy Christian
- Gifted: Understanding My Spiritual Gifts

Find these books and others by Ronald E. Ovitt at Amazon.com

Contents

When I am struggling with…

When I believe I am…

Preface

I have used scriptures all my life to bring me comfort and peace. As a child and growing into young adulthood I had extreme bouts of anxiety and depression. It was the scriptures that brought me consolation and helped me return to joy over and over again. As Christians, we are not left alone with only our imaginations or superstitions to guide us. God has provided a wonderful resource for us to read and follow. It is the Bible. It has been a comfort to millions of people throughout the centuries.

I am passionate about the significance of applying scriptures to our everyday situation. So much so, I decided to take scriptures from the Bible that are relevant to specific life issues and put them into the first person, so you can own them for yourself. It is as if you are saying the verses and personally owning them. You are reading them as if they applied to you, and indeed they do. The goal is that reading Bible verses in this personal form, the truth of the verse will become part of your belief system. This paraphrase is not to be used in place of the actual translation of the verse. If a particular verse really speaks to your heart, go to your favorite Bible translation and read the verse in its full context so you can benefit from the full message and intent of the author.

James admonishes believers: "Be doers of the Word, not just hearers" (James 1:22). Jesus Himself said, "Blessed are all who hear the Word of God and put it into practice" (Luke 11:28). The Apostle Paul wrote to Timothy, "All Scripture is inspired by God and is useful to teach us what is true and to make us realize what is wrong in our lives. It corrects us when we are wrong and teaches us to do what is right. God uses it to prepare and equip His people to do every good work" (2 Timothy 3:16-17). Notice what Paul is saying. He is saying that the proper application of God's Word, through the guidance of the Holy Spirit, teaches us what is right.

It also shows us when we are doing wrong. But it doesn't stay there. It corrects us, or shows us how to do the right thing, and then teaches us how to continue to live for Him. I heard it said this way. The Bible shows us the road we should go down, warns us when we get off the road, shows us how to get back on the right road and then continues to help us stay on the road. This is what applying the scriptures will do. It is the same way when we are troubled. The Word of God can help us correct our thinking and emotional response. It can encourage and comfort us. It can direct us to better thinking and behavior.

May God bless you as you apply these scriptures to your situation and may the Holy Spirit use them to comfort you and bring you peace.

Ron Ovitt

Introduction

I have always been interested in helping people emotionally and spiritually. It started as a child with my own issues—I was a phobic child. There were many things that made me fearful. I went through a period of dissociation, fainting spells, and specific phobias that were difficult to overcome. Throughout my childhood, adolescence, and young adulthood, I had IBS and some compulsive behaviors.

For the most part, I was functional. It was my normal. I came to faith at the age of 11 and dedicated myself to God for His service when I was 15. That seemed to help. I was able to get through high school with great grades and was very active socially. Christianity had become a major part of my life. We started a Christian Club at my school, I volunteered at a mission in Detroit two times a week and was part of a Christian singing group. At the age of 20, I became the Executive Director of Limaland Youth for Christ in Lima, Ohio. Early in this ministry, I began suffering from acute anxiety. Again, I was functional but when I wasn't working I was miserable.

The nature of my role included ministering to people with a variety of emotional issues. This responsibility, in combination with my own personal issues, ignited a desire to study human behavior and how Christianity affected it. I began by taking courses and gaining certification in several Christian counseling methods for ministers. I eventually went back to college to learn more.

My post-graduate classes focused on clinical counseling. In my undergraduate program at Trinity International University, I was trained in existential-phenomenological psychology and behaviorism. My graduate study at Wheaton Graduate School focused primarily on cognitive behavioral psychology and I found myself beginning to find answers for my own conditions.

In 2005, while Executive and Missions Pastor at Calvary Church in Orland Park, Illinois, I set out to provide a one-year program to help people with emotional and addiction-related issues. It takes time to change old habits, negative thinking, and false beliefs. My goal was to create a comprehensive program to address emotions and human behavior that was firmly grounded in Christian principles.

Groundbreaking work by Dr. Daniel Siegel and Dr. Allan N. Schore changed everything I knew about psychology. They introduced new studies on the brain and how it affects the mind. This new area of research was later coined as Affective Regulation by Dr. Schore. I became captivated by therapy studies on how emotions work with the physical body. I immersed myself in new discoveries on memory and how it can be used to affect change in old belief systems. I began to study other doctors working in this field, such as Dr. Bessel van der Kolk, Dr. Pete Levine, Dr. Robert Scaer, and Dr. Francine Shapiro. To this integration of brain, mind, and body, I added the spiritual element to create a life-changing program.

Over the last thirteen years, *Emotional Resilience: Living with the Fruit of the Spirit* has grown into a unique program that specifically targets the areas of habits and addiction.

Emotional Resilience

One of the key principles in Emotional Resilience is what I have called Emotional Relearning™. When we were children, our parents projected many of their problems onto us. Projection is where we focus on the faults in others that are dominant in us. So, when something we did reminded them of their own problems, they would react to us. They would be mad at our childish selfishness if, indeed, selfishness was something they got into trouble for. As adults, people project upon us all the time. No problem...we take it with a grain of salt. However, as children, we don't get off that easy. Children don't have the ability to challenge the parent. Instead, the parents' body language, the tone of voice, and other non-verbal communication gives them feedback and forces children to assume that something must be wrong with them. The child assumes they are the reason for their parents' look of anger, disgust, fear, sadness, or whatever emotion is conveyed. Soon we develop a belief system that self-labels us and relentlessly accuses us.

We must learn to re-parent ourselves and rewrite our inner beliefs. One way we can do this by having a relationship with God and with others that is empathic, compassionate, respectful and validating.

As I studied, taught, and wrote on emotional resilience, it soon became apparent that I was dealing with *learned behavior*. The standard approaches have been cognitive in nature. For years, we have taught that when a person has the wrong notion about themselves they just need to know what is true and correct their thinking. This works in many cases. But as I studied and experimented on myself and counseled others, I found that there was a different type of learning. It was a learning that many of the people I was working with experienced. It was learning that came from trauma. It was what I called *emotional learning.* The learning had been reinforced emotionally and tied into the amygdala-based alarm system. It is a right brain learning, not a left brain learning. Logic alone does not solve the problem. It is like trying to convince a beautiful person that thinks they are ugly that they are beautiful. They won't buy it. They have somehow emotionally learned that they are ugly, and even though it is a lie, it is deeply and emotionally believed. A lie about oneself that was emotionally learned can change when the truth is *emotionally relearned.*

THE THREE ER'S OF EMOTIONAL RESILIENCE

The goal of emotional resilience is to bounce back from painful emotions. We teach this in three phases. I call these phases ER's.

PHASE 1: Emotional Recognition. We need to be able to stop and recognize our emotions and when we are over-emoting. We need to feel our emotions and then own feeling them so we can move into the second phase.

PHASE 2: Emotional Regulation. Regulating our emotions allows us to return from painful emotions to love, joy, peace, patience, kindness, goodness, faithfulness, gentleness, and self-control (the Fruit of the Spirit). We have a choice. We can choose to regulate our emotions. We can learn to move from hypervigilance— constantly scanning our environment for threats—to a more calming presence. In this phase, we are cognitively aware that these negative feelings are due to faulty wiring from lies that we believed in the past. It is a false alarm. When we understand that we're receiving a false alarm, we can ride out the emotional feeling and watch it dissipate. When we learn how to regulate our emotions, we are ready for the third ER.

PHASE 3: Emotional Relearning™. In Phase Three, we emotionally revisit a time (memory) when we felt the same way we're feeling now. These memories often house the early emotional roots of the core beliefs behind the feeling we're experiencing. Many times, these beliefs are lies about who we are, and the life predictions associated with those beliefs are often erroneous. It is in these memories that we can discover what we are believing and challenge them with the truth. When the source of this truth is authoritative, such as God, a loving grandparent, or a wiser self, then the truth is believed both cognitively and emotionally. When the truth is relearned emotionally (like the original lie), the lie is changed forever!

YOUR EMOTIONAL SELF IMAGE

For many of us, how we view ourselves is often learned in childhood. It was modeled for us by our caregivers in the way they treated us and perceived us. What they did, what they said, and their body language all gave us impressions and started us down a road of self-image and beliefs. It could also be what they did not do—uncelebrated birthdays, missed events, or long periods away from home can also send negative messages.

When mixed with generally positive messages, children have the capacity to understand that occasional parental outbursts or erratic behavior are an exception to the rule. But when negative messages are constant, the child starts to wonder what is wrong with themselves. In these cases, immature beliefs emerge with no one to help correct them.

These beliefs are *learned emotionally* and if we are to overcome these beliefs, we need to emotionally *relearn* the truth. One of the ways that we can emotionally relearn who we are is through God's Word. That is why we have created the *Power Up!* book series.

Through Bible paraphrase affirmations and scriptural prayers, with repetition, the Holy Spirit is able to take the Word and emotionally renew our minds.

Understanding You

As we come to the Bible for truth, it is good to know what we believe about ourselves that may need to be changed. We may be believing lies about ourselves and that the emotional result of those beliefs is faulty wiring. What we are feeling may be a false alarm generated from erroneous beliefs. But don't think this will be easy. Often, we don't know why we are reacting.

Many of the memories from trauma are *implicit* (out of conscious awareness) and are carried forward from the past. Instead, the amygdala—the brain's alarm center—looks for warning signs developed in our brains as children to protect us. These triggers include body language, the tone of voice, certain phrases or smells, and many other cues. As a result of these triggers or cues, our bodies react to these trigger sensations before our brains understand why. These sensations are actually emotions. The word *emotion* comes from the root words "to move." The trigger sensation makes us move and the resulting emotion is described as a *feeling*.

When we recognize trigger sensations in our body (Phase 1 ER), we are able to stop and regulate them (Phase 2 ER). We do this by understanding that they are false alarms and by realizing that we don't have to listen to them. Once we are calmed, we return to the feeling, identify the beliefs behind our reaction, emotionally relearn the truth, and change the lie (Phase 3 ER)—Emotional Relearning™. To accomplish this, we need to become aware of where we are emotionally and what some of our beliefs are.

The more honest we can be about our own maturity needs, the more we can seek change.

SOUL YEARNINGS

The human infant is one of the most vulnerable of all creatures with tremendous needs that must be taken care of. A baby cannot see, feed itself, or move around on its own. It can't think or seeks its own protection. A baby can only cry, alerting others that they need assistance. Physically, the baby must be fed, cleaned up after, and protected from all danger. However, as a human grows older, they are able to take care of many of these needs themselves. Of course, not all of our needs are physical. We also have soul needs—emotional and spiritual needs that are important to our self-image and its survival. When our soul needs are unmet, they become soul yearnings:

- **Safety.** To be safe and comforted.
- **Purpose.** To have a personal purpose.
- **Belonging.** To know that you belong.
- **Significance.** To be significant and have honor.
- **Love.** To be loved and known as lovable.

When these soul needs are not fulfilled, they cause emotional conflict. They leave strongholds of doubt, fear, and longings that lurk in our hearts. We find ourselves believing lies about ourselves and trying various ways of escaping the emotional pain they create. For this, we need emotional resilience—the ability to bounce back from emotional pain. We are full of emotions. We can't get away from them. However, the goal is not to avoid emotions, it is to regulate them.

YOUR PERSONAL JOURNEY

Children have different needs at various stages of their development. If these needs are met, we move on to maturity. If they are not met, we struggle with maturity and growing into adulthood.

Power Up! includes four self-assessments about your personal journey. In this section, assess your childhood development, your adult maturity, and your current emotional maturity. In the next section, assess any immature beliefs you may have.

SELF-ASSESSMENT #1: Childhood Development

INSTRUCTIONS: Read each statement below describing basic childhood needs. Using the rating scale provided, circle the rating that best describes how you felt as a child regarding each statement.

1=not true for me | 3=somewhat true for me | 5=very true for me

As a child...

I felt safety and security with those I trusted and loved.	1 2 3 4 5
I knew that love is constant, unconditional, and always there no matter what.	1 2 3 4 5
I knew I was loved, special, valued, and unique.	1 2 3 4 5
I had the capacity to return to peace and joy from painful emotions.	1 2 3 4 5
I knew that I belonged and was connected to others in a special way.	1 2 3 4 5
I felt loved for who I was without having to perform.	1 2 3 4 5
I had a bond with our Creator and life in His Spirit.	1 2 3 4 5
I had purpose, meaning, and freedom to use my strengths for good.	1 2 3 4 5
I knew that it is never too late to have caring and nurturing relationships.	1 2 3 4 5

NOTES: _____

_____

_____

_____

_____

SELF-ASSESSMENT #2: Adult Maturity

INSTRUCTIONS: Read each statement below and rate your current maturity. Using the rating scale provided, circle the rating that best describes you as an adult regarding each statement.

I am very immature—1 2 3 4 5 6 7 8 9 10—*I am very mature*

As an adult...

I handle my emotions.	1 2 3 4 5 6 7 8 9 10
I fulfill my responsibilities.	1 2 3 4 5 6 7 8 9 10
I live with relationships.	1 2 3 4 5 6 7 8 9 10
I am assertive in a healthy way.	1 2 3 4 5 6 7 8 9 10
I say no to unhealthy boundaries.	1 2 3 4 5 6 7 8 9 10
I handle intimidation by others.	1 2 3 4 5 6 7 8 9 10
I handle pressure to be a people-pleaser.	1 2 3 4 5 6 7 8 9 10
I delay gratification.	1 2 3 4 5 6 7 8 9 10

NOTES: _____

_____

_____

_____

_____

_____

_____

_____

_____

_____

_____

_____

_____

_____

SELF-ASSESSMENT #3: Emotional Maturity

INSTRUCTIONS: There are seven categories of emotional maturity. Read the descriptions for each category on the following pages. Using the rating scale provided, circle the rating that best describes your current emotional maturity in each category.

I am very immature—1 2 3 4 5 6 7 8 9 10—*I am very mature*

1. LOVE

Immature. An immature person is insecure in their relationships and craves love and acceptance. They are clingy and needy, not secure in who they are in the eyes of others. The need is so high that they almost demand affection and love. Fear of rejection and abandonment drives them to try hard and to please others. They feel they must avoid any sign of weakness and often put on a front, so people won't know who they really are. Ironically, when love, affection, or praise is given, it is hard for an immature person to receive it and is often unaccepted.

Mature. For a mature person, love is sharing with others. There is a sense of seeing ourselves as an adult that is on equal footing with other adults. Different? Yes. Different skill levels? Yes. But an inferior, lower class adult? No. Therefore, they do not have a problem receiving or sharing love, free to be vulnerable and open to others. They do not fear rejection or have an incessant need to please people.

I am very immature—1 2 3 4 5 6 7 8 9 10—*I am very mature*

NOTES: _____

_____

_____

_____

2. EMOTIONS

Immature. When we haven't received the love that we needed as a child, we stay immature in our emotions as an adult. We find it difficult to handle frustration or criticism. We fear rejection and abandonment. We have low ego-strength and are easily crushed in spirit. We can become jealous, angry, and unwilling to forgive what we feel are personal wounds. We have fluctuating moods—from being aloof to temper tantrums. Ironically, emotional turmoil seems normal and we fear change even if it could be so much better.

Mature. When we are mature, we understand that emotions are not to be shunned or avoided. We realize that everyone has emotions—they are byproducts of sensations that produce chemical reactions in our brains. When these sensations occur, we experience a wave of emotion. As mature people, we see that our emotions don't have to define us. We can view emotions as a wave with an ebb and flow that will soon dissipate. From this objective vantage, we can perceive emotions as signals that something might be wrong. Rather than avoiding or simply reacting to them, we can "ride the wave," assess the experience afterward, and, if needed, look for solutions.

I am very immature—1 2 3 4 5 6 7 8 9 10—*I am very mature*

NOTES: _____

_____

_____

_____

_____

_____

_____

_____

_____

_____

3. RESPONSIBILITY

Immature. When we are immature. it is easy to procrastinate, focus on other things, avoid, or simply deny responsibility. The fear of failure (and sometimes success) can sabotage our best of intentions. It is easy to blame circumstances, others, or emotional turmoil as a reason for not fulfilling our duties. It is easier to find excuses and try to make it through emotionally than it is to try to do a job and fail at it. Negative self-beliefs, lack of confidence, and fear of rejection play havoc with our performance.

Mature. When we are mature, we are aware of our commitments and their consequences. We have confidence and a plan that will help us do what we said we would do. We know that there will be problems and, when they occur, we confront them and look for solutions. We have high integrity and choose the best win-win solution.

I am very immature—1 2 3 4 5 6 7 8 9 10—*I am very mature*

NOTES: _____

_____
_____
_____
_____
_____
_____
_____
_____
_____
_____
_____
_____
_____
_____

4. WIN-WIN

Immature. When we are immature, we have not learned to share, delay gratification, or be willing to take risks. It is hard to give up control for fear of negative consequences. If things fall in our favor, we may be willing to give, but not to take. Or the opposite could be true—we are willing to take, but not to give. Compromise and win-win leave us too vulnerable.

Mature. Maturity means that we are secure in who we are and do not need to prove our worth. It is not about saving face, putting on a mask, or staying ahead of fear. Instead, we can take things in stride and work toward everyone winning. We care for ourselves, but we also deeply care for others. We give money, time, or effort to help those we love and care for. Finally, we are able to receive from others, too. Though we do not strive to get attention and recognition, we do not fear it either. We take things in stride and are thankful for our blessings and the abilities God has given us.

I am very immature—1 2 3 4 5 6 7 8 9 10—*I am very mature*

NOTES: _____

_____
_____
_____
_____
_____
_____
_____
_____
_____
_____
_____

5. RESILIENCE

Immature. When we are immature, it is difficult to bounce back from painful emotions. We would rather fight, run, or just give up. All of these are easier than facing our emotions. We find it hard to assess what is wrong and how to fix it. Instead, we ignore the situation, blame others, or procrastinate. Through avoidance, we escape painful emotions by distracting ourselves with other things that seem to make us feel good. Deep down, we find it easy to blame fate, luck, or even God for our situations. When we are immature, we do not take personal responsibility for our emotions.

Mature. When we are mature, we know that emotions happen, and life is a learning experience. We accept responsibility and learn from feedback, allowing us to return from painful emotions to peace and joy. We take on an optimistic view of life and put our faith and hope in God. We move on from negative experiences and look for more positive opportunities.

I am very immature—1 2 3 4 5 6 7 8 9 10—*I am very mature*

NOTES: _____

_____

_____

_____

_____

_____

_____

_____

_____

_____

_____

_____

_____

_____

6. STRESS

Immature. When we are immature, we do not know how to handle stress. We avoid the reality of our situation until we are cornered and must react. At that point, pressure is built up and we find it easy to be critical, pessimistic, angry, and anxious. Instead of attacking the problem, we find it easier to attack people.

Mature. When we are mature, we feel good about who we are. We are confident in our abilities and optimistic about potential outcomes. We do not fear other peoples' reactions or exaggerate negative outcomes. We have realistic views of the risks involved and are able to assess and make plans to remedy the situation we are facing. We are relaxed and confident in our ability to overcome stressful situations.

*I am very immature—*1 2 3 4 5 6 7 8 9 10*—I am very mature*

NOTES: _____

_____

_____

_____

_____

_____

_____

_____

_____

_____

_____

_____

_____

_____

_____

_____

_____

7. RELATIONSHIPS

Immature. When we are immature, we live with fear bonds rather than love bonds. Fear is an evil taskmaster, making us easily influenced by the whims of anyone who is good at manipulating through fear and intimidation. What they don't do to us, we do to ourselves. We believe we are no good, a failure, helpless, thought poorly of and walking on thin ice that could crack under us at any moment. This negative belief system is comprehensive. According to the stress level and history of our relationship experiences, we can vacillate between being indecisive or overly rushing to judgment. We can be clingy with others or want nothing to do with others. It is easy to become codependent. We can be overly sensitive to the criticism from others and yet be hypercritical of them. We will not take responsibility for own actions or deficiencies but will blame others for our circumstances.

Mature. When we are mature, we have a healthy independence and yet are good team players, as required. We know how to be cooperative and yet stand our ground on important issues. We treat others with respect and have patience toward them. We are secure in who we are and do not fear the erroneous opinions of others. We are respectful of others and have good healthy boundaries. We know how to say, "no" yet still be cooperative and work toward the common good. We are socially responsible. We have a good balance between social relationships and time alone. We exercise empathy and compassion toward others without becoming codependent.

I am very immature—1 2 3 4 5 6 7 8 9 10—*I am very mature*

NOTES: _____

_____

_____

_____

_____

_____

IMMATURE BELIEFS

Immaturity is being locked into childhood interpretations of traumatic events that may be distortions of reality because they were adopted when we were emotionally immature. Negative, self-defeating beliefs about life, relationships, ourselves, and God that we experience as adults are lies, half-truths, and immature beliefs that we may have adopted as children. These distortions affect our worldview and predictions about outcomes, stunting our ability to be mature in life situations. These distortions need to be challenged and dwelt with over time.

Complete the next assessment to see if you have immature self-beliefs you emotionally learned as a child that may be causing or contributing to current emotional issues.

SELF-ASSESSMENT #4: Immature Beliefs

INSTRUCTIONS: Read the statements below describing basic immature beliefs. Checkmark the ones you struggle with.

☐ Others must approve of me or else I am bad.

☐ I am an inferior person.

☐ I must please others to be liked.

☐ I am bad if I speak my mind and disagree.

☐ I must not question authority.

☐ I must get permission from others.

☐ I cannot fail or else I am no good.

☐ My feelings are not important.

☐ I will never succeed.

☐ I must do what I am told.

☐ If I disagree, I am wrong.

☐ I cannot do it by myself.

☐ I am not capable to manage on my own.

☐ Feelings are not important.

☐ I will never be good enough.

☐ It is bad to be average.

☐ I must be liked.

☐ Other people's opinions are more important than mine.

☐ I must not fail.

☐ I must hide my mistakes.

☐ Things are easy for others.

☐ My beliefs aren't as important as yours.

☐ I cannot trust others to do what they say.

☐ Others are not as afraid, mad, or sad as I am.

☐ I must be nice to everyone.

☐ I must stay in control.

☐ If I do wrong, I will be abandoned.

☐ I must do it myself.

☐ I will always let others down.

☐ Others will always let me down.

☐ I cannot choose my own values.

☐ It is a disgrace to lose.

☐ If I disagree, I will be banished.

☐ If people knew the real me, they would reject me.

☐ Conflict is dangerous for me.

☐ If I please others, I will be liked.

☐ I cannot say what is on my mind.

☐ If I get angry, I will lose control.

☐ If I do what they say, I will not be rejected.

THE IMPACT OF IMMATURE BELIEFS

When soul yearnings are not fulfilled during childhood, strongholds of doubt, fear, and longings often linger, influencing our worldview as adults.

- Fear of failure
- Feeling inferior to other adults
- An urgent need to please others
- Fear of abandonment and rejection
- Inordinate guilt
- Anxiety
- Feelings of being broken and shameful
- Fear of expressing self
- Fear of God
- Overly competitive

When we believe distortions of the truth that were learned emotionally as a child, we often try various ways of escaping the emotional pain they create.

Let God Heal Your Emotions

The purpose of this book is to help you heal your emotions by letting the Holy Spirit use the Word of God to renew your mind and transform you into the person He created you to be. We do this by allowing the Bible and our relationship with God to help us to combat the emotional lies we believe about ourselves and relearn the truth about who we are in Christ.

Here are the three phases of Emotional Relearning™ in more detail so you can learn how to let Biblical affirmations help change your beliefs.

ER 1: EMOTIONAL RECOGNITION

If we are going to break out of this vicious cycle, we need to become aware of when we are being triggered so we can change it before we habitually react.

Emotional Triggers. Everyday occurrences can trigger deep-seated beliefs about ourselves when they recall implicit (out of awareness) memories which are laden with sensations that our amygdala previously registered. When a look or feeling recalls a painful memory or belief about ourselves, it sets off a right-brain alarm and we go into an immediate fight, flight, freeze, or fix mode. Some of those right brain triggers are:

- Looks of disgust, rejection, sadness, anger, or hurt
- Let down expectations
- Angry body language
- Negative tone of voice
- Abandonment
- Over expectations

- Being put down, mocked, degraded
- Unforgiveness
- Threats
- Blank stare
- Favoritism or comparison to someone else
- Smothering or overprotection

Outward Triggers. Outward triggers are reactions to cues due to negative false beliefs. Many times, these triggers are missed by our consciousness and go straight to our physical bodies as sensations. If we can learn to become aware of body cues, we can retrace our steps and make sense of what is going on inside our minds.

- What happened?
- How did I react?
- What thoughts went through my mind?
- How am I feeling emotionally?
- Did I feel validated, respected, heard, and loved?
- If not, am I holding in anger and frustration?
- Am I being passive when I really feel more aggressive?

Inward Reactions to Triggers. Many times, our bodies react to triggers well before our minds realize what is going on. These sensations can cause us to react with emotion. We can learn to be aware of physical symptoms that may indicate that there is a false belief in play. Our bodies react quickly to deceptive brain messages.

- Tension headache
- Migraine
- Sore back or neck
- Irritable bowel

- Tightness in chest
- Downward mood
- Butterflies in stomach
- Tired
- Lethargic
- Agitation
- Recurrent pain
- Increased desire to escape through illicit means
- Migraine pressure

Our bodies react much quicker than our brains to deceptive brain messages. When chronic pain, irritable bowel, daily headaches, aching neck, or tiredness are normal, we may never stop to think that those symptoms could be a reaction to habitual painful thinking. Hypervigilance may be causing us to experience increased anxiety from sustained and heightened sensory awareness. This might be easy to miss. Why? First, because these symptoms have become our norm. Second, because we're coping, we're getting by. We tend to feel that coping is taking care of the situation, but it isn't. It is only perpetuating it. It is like worrying. Worrying doesn't actually do anything about a situation—it doesn't fix anything.

It's natural to react to a fear-based alarm with hypervigilance but, like worry, it doesn't resolve the problem. As our bodies react to triggers, we need to pause and tune into our body sensations. We need to ask ourselves:

- Why is this happening?
- Why is this happening now?
- What am I feeling while this is going on?
- What am I believing about myself at this moment?

ER 2: EMOTIONAL REGULATION

As we become aware of our reactions, whether it is mental, physical, or emotional, we can begin to regulate our reaction.

Emotional Vertigo™. Where does this hypervigilance come from? It comes as a reaction to a fear-based trigger. The brain interprets the initial fear signal as an imperative for action—you must do something! It is as if you have received a threatening phone call and someone is coming to get you. It is like the feeling of having a predator in the room with you. Airplane pilots sometimes experience vertigo, or what is called spatial disorientation—a state of temporary spatial confusion resulting from misleading information sent to the brain by various sensory organs. The body's navigational system works well on the ground, but in an aircraft, during sudden acceleration or radial flight, it can trick a pilot into feeling like they are ascending when they are descending. The pilot must fight the urge to panic and must not give in to this wrong information. They have been trained to believe that, under certain conditions, their senses can be wrong. That is exactly what happens when you experience a stress reaction—you're having *emotional* vertigo.

Regulate Emotional Vertigo™. Just like the trained airplane pilot, to overcome this false alarm you must be willing to believe that, under certain conditions, your senses can be wrong. Pilots are trained to recognize it as a deceptive message, ignore it, and follow protocol. There are many techniques and protocols that we teach to overcome this problem. But first, you must deal with the sensation itself. You must know and believe that it is a faulty message. After all, it is only a sensation. It will not hurt you. It will dissipate. It is from faulty wiring. It's a false alarm.

Bouncing back, being resilient. The goal of emotional regulation is to be able to bounce back from painful emotions. We want to regulate elevated sensations and return to homeostasis. This ability to bounce back should have been taught in childhood; however, many of us never acquired the skill. It is not too late! The good news is that we can learn to be resilient today.

Return to peace and joy. How can we return to peace and joy from painful thoughts, emotions, and sensations? There are five steps you need to take when painful emotions take over:

1. Breathe and relax through it.
2. Ride the wave.
3. Create healthy distractions.
4. Catch yourself succeeding.
5. Pursue the Fruit of the Spirit.

STEP 1: Breathe and relax through it. One way you can extinguish a stressful urge is to relax and take a deep breath. When you are reacting in fear, remind yourself that it is an amygdala-driven false alarm. The amygdala is the part of the emotional center (limbic) of the brain that serves as a "guard shack," watching over and warning you of impending danger. In the brain, an amygdala-driven alarm is calmed down through the parasympathetic nervous system. You can override the misinformation of an alarm by learning to relax and deep breath when the amygdala warns you of danger. You can fight the urge to panic; you can avoid giving in to this wrong information just as the pilot learns to ignore vertigo. Relax...and your body will follow. At the onset of hypervigilance, train your body to relax. Retrain the brain to use its parasympathetic nervous system to slow your heart rate and lower your blood pressure once a false alarm has been sounded.

25

STEP 2: Ride the wave. Another way to manage painful thoughts, emotions, and sensations is to think of it as a wave. Here it comes! But, it is only a wave and you have the perfect boogie board. Now…just ride the wave. Let it take you up, forward, toward the shore—faster, faster, slower, slower, to the shallow waters. Finally, it is gone…dissipated onto the shore. Do this with your sensation. Remember that like an ocean's wave—it will not last. Commit to riding it out. Ignore it and watch it go away.

STEP 3: Create healthy distractions. Remember that painful thoughts, emotions, and sensations are a stimulus that you can ride out or contain. It is not a question of whether we are going to distract ourselves or not. It is how healthy will the distraction be? When the false alarm comes, the first thing we want to do is escape the emotional pain. The same part of our brain that registers physical pain lights up when we are triggered by a false alarm, therefore, we try to escape. Escapes are any of the following used to excess to distract yourself from the fearful sensation you are feeling:

E	Excitement
S	Substance
C	Compulsive Behavior
A	Avoidance
P	People
E	Emotionalism
S	Sex

Instead of escaping, learn to stay with the sensation, use breathing techniques, and ride the wave using healthy distractions until the sensation dissipates. It is hard to continue our deep breathing or ride the wave of emotion if we are constantly ruminating about the fears we have or if we are using an unhealthy escape. To help ourselves, we need to be deliberate in the way we handle irrational onslaughts of thoughts and emotions. When it comes to irrational habits, a great deal has been studied and taught by Jeffery Swartz and his study on OCD behavior. There are three things that we can do to help us get through this momentary discomfort and create healthy distractions.

- **Call it what it is.** When you get the sensation, it feels like an emergency. You *must do* something! But the truth is, it is only a false alarm! It is not real. You must realize that the alarm you're feeling is false so that you can make a change. It seems counterintuitive to ignore an alarm, but trust me—if you were forced to leave your office eight times in one day because of faulty wiring in your company's fire alarm system, you would quickly get over the panic. We need to begin to call these alarming feelings what they are—"faulty wiring." They are learned behaviors based on lies. Therefore, you need to learn *new* behaviors associated with the alarm. Remember it is a false alarm; you are not going to die! You want to treat it much like you would the wind blowing against your outside window. Even if it startles you, it only takes a few seconds to realize that all is well and there is no danger.

- **Confirm that you don't have to listen to it or do what it urges you to do.** Nail biting is an irrational reaction to a sensation in the fingernails. A more sensible reaction is to rub them on a piece of clothing and ignore the temptation to bite them. As the nails grow, the sensation dissipates, and you take care of your nails normally. There is no logical reason to bite your nails. So, when you sense the stimulus, instead of thinking "I *must*," think in terms of "I don't *have* to." The urge to bite your nails is faulty wiring. You don't have to react to this urge any more than you would need to respond to a faulty smoke detector that you know is broken and is emitting a warning when there is obviously no smoke or fire. Instead of reacting to danger, get busy fixing the actual problem—override the faulty wiring. Get rid of the stimulus and extinguish the alarm through an acceptable method of behavior. Remember that when you are reacting and are tempted to escape your emotional pain, the urge you feel is *faulty wiring.* Just like vertigo, there is no real danger. Even though the alarm urges you to react, you can ignore it. Like the trained pilot, you need to fight the urge to panic and remember that under certain conditions, your senses can be wrong.

- **Distract yourself.** The next step is to distract yourself. Not with ESCAPES, but with *healthy* distractions. Who do you trust that knows about your situation? Give them a call and ask for their support. There are many helpful, positive things you can do that will allow your brain to relax and return to a more comfortable state. What do you like to read? What hobby have you always wanted to take up? What courses would you enjoy? What self-help books can you find? Using this book and meditating on the scripture affirmations that apply to your emotional state is a great distraction. Identify your interests and develop them. Stepping toward a healthy distraction that you really enjoy helps diminish the trigger. The way we counter such an emotional belief is to have a source of truth that is credible enough to believe and powerful enough to overcome the source of the lie.

STEP 4: Catch yourself succeeding. When painful emotions arise, we often turn to cravings (habits and addictions) to escape. When you successfully ignore those cravings and ride out the sensation, you need to celebrate! Replay your success again and again—you did it! Feel it...relive it...replay it. Congratulate yourself! This is retraining your brain so the prefrontal cortex, the executive center of your brain, will get the message and overrule the amygdala in the future.

STEP 5: Pursue the Fruit of the Spirit. The Bible talks about the byproduct of Christian spirituality—the Fruit of the Spirit. Paul writes this:

> "The Holy Spirit produces this kind of fruit in our lives: love, joy, peace, patience, kindness, goodness, faithfulness, gentleness, and self-control" (Galatians 5:22-23).

The Fruit of the Spirit is the key to achieving Emotional Resilience. As you focus on biblical truth and grow spiritually, you will develop the ability to return from painful emotions and achieve love, joy, peace, patience, kindness, goodness, faithfulness, gentleness, and self-control. The Fruit of the Spirit is how we regulate our emotions.

ER 3: EMOTIONAL RELEARNING™

Emotional Relearning™ is the practice of correcting a lie about ourselves by learning the truth emotionally. The lie was emotionally learned and feels true. This is not due to the logic of the belief—it is based on the enormous emotion carried with that belief. The way we counter that distortion is to have a source of truth that is credible enough to believe and powerful enough to overcome the source of the lie.

Let's consider an example of a father yelling at a child in rage: "What's wrong with you? You are no good; I wish you had never been born!" The parent's tone of voice, the facial expression, body language, the words spoken, and the authority behind the person saying it would result in the child believing that there is something wrong with them—they are, indeed, no good. This belief would be cognitively learned, emotionally reinforced, and tied into the amygdala-based alarm system. Because the father has the power and authority to do something horrible about the child being no good, the child would experience immense fright. That fear would become embedded in the child's emotions, creating feelings of danger about what might happen if they aren't careful and don't please people.

We can counter negative, emotionally-learned lies through a source of truth that is credible enough to believe and powerful enough to overcome the source of the lie.

When a credible source corrects the awful lie that we believe about ourselves and shares the truth with us with authority, it is an emotionally moving experience. It is liberating! It is exhilarating! God can and will do this for you. He is the final authority. What God believes about you trumps all the lies that were reinforced by other people and circumstances in your life.

Through the personalized Bible verses in this book, God will reinforce the truth to you as you read, pray, and meditate on His Word. How does this work? There are six steps to Emotional Relearning™:

STEP 1: Know what you are feeling. The first step is to stop as soon as you recognize that you are over-emoting. Name the sensation or emotion you are feeling at that moment. This also works after the fact. If you had an emotional episode last week, reflect on that experience, think about it, and name the sensation or emotion you experienced.

STEP 2: Know what you are believing about yourself. Once you know what you are feeling, ask yourself, "What am I believing about myself." Your belief may be true; it may not be true. For example, "I am a piece of garbage" is an emotional belief, but it is not true. "My mom did not love me" may, to some extent, be true. It happens. However, true or false, what was the consequence of that belief? Chances are, that belief, whether true or not true, caused you to feel you were in danger of not having your soul needs met—the basic emotional and spiritual needs that are important to our self-image and its survival. When the feeling of safety, purpose, belonging, significance or love is unmet or threatened, it can elicit a primal "I'm going to die!" type of reaction that is believed emotionally. The fact is, you did not die. And you won't die now either. But the consequences of what we learned emotionally and believed as children often remain intact, leaving us with strongholds of doubt and fear as we get older. These beliefs often become integrated into our adult self-image. Even now, when a look or feeling recalls a painful memory or belief about ourselves, it sets off a right-brain alarm and we go into an immediate fight, flight, freeze, or fix mode.

STEP 3: Examine what you believe about yourself. Once you identify the negative belief you developed as a child, examine it. Calm yourself down and begin to examine exactly what you are believing. Be your own observer—a detective with an objective view. Make sure you have an accurate grasp on the negative belief.

STEP 4: Invite God to share the truth with you. This is deeply spiritual. God loves you and knows the truth about you. Invite Him to share the truth with you. This is not the time to rush. Focus; wait and let God speak to your heart. You can do this by reading the affirmations, meditations, and Bible verses provided in this book. Linger with them; pray and let them sink in. God is omnipresent and knows you intimately. He can and will share the truth with you. He can do this in many ways. As you read the resources in this book, an insight may come to you. As you pray, you might sense God is with you. As you meditate on what you read and see yourself living with this new truth, God may affirm the truth through your senses. Everyone is different. The goal is to let God share the truth with you. If at this time, you are not able to connect spiritually in this way, do not be discouraged. There are other sources of truth to draw from. (It could be argued that all truth is God's truth.) For example, ask yourself what someone who knows you well and loves you (perhaps a loving grandmother) say? What would your mature wise self say to someone else in this situation? What truth would a trusted friend offer? Ask God to help you search for the truth from a credible source. Jesus said it best: "You will know the truth and the truth will set you free" (John 8:32, *New Living Translation*).

STEP 5: Consider the truth and listen for disbelief. Once you receive some truth, think about it. Dwell on it. Try saying it out loud. When you do, watch for a fearful response, disbelief, or a sense of rejection. We don't give up beliefs without a fight. The lies we believe about ourselves are strongholds coming from wounds that were emotionally learned and are emotionally believed. That means they cause an emotional reaction rather than being based on logical reasoning. A phobia is a good example. Try telling someone that is claustrophobic that it is safe to use the elevator. Their phobic fear will fight them from getting on the elevator. Their emotions will argue with them. Likewise, when you are trying to contradict a long-standing negative belief about yourself and neutralize the danger signal it creates, you will get pushback. This is good! Why? It is good because it indicates that you have progressed from responding with a kneejerk reaction to challenging a negative belief and considering an alternative belief. This is the first step toward creating a new healthy belief about yourself! Once you start this inner dialog, you have a strong chance of continuing it. Learn to renounce the lie and pronounce the truth. We have provided you with some examples on the following pages.

RENOUNCE THE LIE...
I am worthless, and I have no significance.

PRONOUNCE THE TRUTH...
I am God's child.

"But to all who believed him and accepted him, he gave the right to become children of God" (John 1:12).

RENOUNCE THE LIE...
It's too late, and I cannot change.

PRONOUNCE THE TRUTH...
I am a new creation in Christ.

"Let the Spirit renew your thoughts and attitudes. Put on your new nature, created to be like God—truly righteous and holy" (Ephesians 4:23-24).

RENOUNCE THE LIE...
I am bad, unforgivable, rejected by God and man.

PRONOUNCE THE TRUTH...
There is no condemnation for those who know Christ as Savior.

"There is no condemnation for those who belong to Christ Jesus. And because you belong to him, the power of the life-giving Spirit has freed you from the power of sin that leads to death" (Romans 8:1-2).

> **RENOUNCE THE LIE...**
> I am unlovable and unwanted.
>
> **PRONOUNCE THE TRUTH...**
> I am deeply loved by Jesus.
>
> *(Jesus speaking) "I have loved you even as the Father has loved me. Remain in my love" (John 15:9).*

> **RENOUNCE THE LIE...**
> I am nobody, and I have no significance.
>
> **PRONOUNCE THE TRUTH...**
> I am born again and entitled to great spiritual blessings because of God's love for me.
>
> *"All praise to God, the Father of our Lord Jesus Christ, who has blessed us with every spiritual blessing in the heavenly realms because we are united with Christ" (Ephesians 1:3).*

> **RENOUNCE THE LIE...**
> My life is meaningless, and I have no purpose.
>
> **PRONOUNCE THE TRUTH...**
> I am God's ambassador created to do His will on earth by doing good.
>
> *"God saved you by his grace when you believed. And you can't take credit for this; it is a gift from God. Salvation is not a reward for the good things we have done, so none of us can boast about it. For we are God's masterpiece. He has created us anew in Christ Jesus, so we can do the good things he planned for us long ago" (Ephesians 2:8-10).*

STEP 6: Affirm the new truth. You received a new truth about yourself. If it came from God, then you know you can trust it. Now it is a matter of continuously reinforcing it emotionally and logically until it becomes second nature. In this step, scriptures, prayer, and meditation are especially helpful. Reading and meditating on Bible verses will assure you of the presence of a loving Heavenly Father who loves you, protects you, and will help re-parent you with correct beliefs about who you are.

Using the Resource Section

It would be easy to just read these verses when you feel the need. In a way, that is why I wrote this personal resource—to be a help in the time of need. But if all you do is read through the verses, you will be missing the depth of experience you can have. Move beyond a casual reading of the Word and into a deep belief in your heart.

PRAY, THEN READ IT

Something spurred you to pick up this book. It isn't a novel or textbook—it is a collection of scripture to comfort and motivate you when you sense you need help. Therefore, the chances are that you will come to this book with a burden on your heart, looking for help. I encourage you to talk to God before you begin reading the following Bible verses. Ask the Holy Spirit to help you, speak to you, comfort you, and guide you through these resources. Ask Him to open your mind and heart to receive what God has for you.

BELIEVE IT

It is easy to read the verses in this book and yet go away untouched. That is part of the reason I took each verse and rewrote it as an affirmation. I want you to believe the verses for yourself. I want you to read the verse and application and say, "I believe it." At that moment you either will accept it or there will be a twinge of doubt or, perhaps, much stronger. If this happens, you will know in your heart that there is a problem. This is okay!! Why? Because recognizing doubt is the beginning of accepting it as truth.

If you sense a twinge of doubt, stop. Tell God about it. Say something like this: "Lord, I am having a hard time believing this. You know my heart. Please help my unbelief." Next, you want to receive the truth by faith.

RECEIVE IT

Receiving truth is an act of faith. It is saying, "Lord, I don't feel that this is true right now, but those are just my feelings. I come now and pronounce that it is true by faith and receive it in Jesus' name." Doing two more things will cement this truth in your mind and body—visualize it and feel it in your body.

SEE IT

What would it feel like to believe the verse? How would you act? What thoughts would you have about yourself and how would you relate to others if this verse was true? Take a moment and visualize yourself living as though that verse is true for you. See it and believe it as you live it on the screen of your mind.

BREATHE IT

You can say you believe something but if your body doesn't buy it, the body will win every time. That is why I encourage you to expand what you have believed, received, and visualized into your actual physical experience. Take a deep breathe in and let it out. Relax and take in a deep breath; as you exhale, start to read the verse. Accept it into your physical and mental self in this relaxed state. Feel the comfort, affirmation, and the significance it brings to you. Breath again. As you exhale, thank God for the truth you have just affirmed. Accept it by faith.

These steps help take you from a casual reading to meditation that God can use to speak deep into your heart and help you to understand and apply it in your daily life.

It is our prayer that these scriptural affirmations will help you emotionally believe the truth about you and how deeply loved by God you are!

WHEN I NEED...

Comfort
Courage
Guidance
Forgiveness/Salvation
Hope/ Patience
Love for Others
Peace
Self-control Over Addictions/Habits
Strength
Anxiety
Trust

Comfort

Almighty God, You give me strength. You are my God. You save me. You are my Heavenly Father. I will praise and exalt You (Exodus 15:2).

The joy of the Lord is my strength (Nehemiah 8:10).

I am full of courage, secure and confident because there is hope in You, my God. I find safety all around me and I rest in You (Job 11:18).

You can see what kind of love God the Father has showered me with, so much so that I am called a child of God (1 John 3:1).

I lie down and sleep because You alone, Lord, make me safe (Psalm 4:8).

I trust in God's unfailing love. I rejoice because He rescues me. I sing praises to the Lord because He is good to me (Psalm 13:5-6).

I must refrain from anger and turn away from being hateful. I need to stop fretting—it only leads to evil (Psalm 37:8).

God is with me even when I am walking through the darkest trials of my life. Therefore, I will not fear, I am never alone. Like a loving shepherd with His tender sheep, His rod and staff protect me and bring me comfort (Psalm 23:4).

It is true that God's pursues me with His goodness and His unfailing love every day of my life (Psalm 23:6).

Lord, in my heart I have heard You say, "Come, talk with me." My heart shouts, "Yes, Lord, I am coming!" (Psalm 27:8).

I rejoice in God's unfailing love, for He sees my troubles and cares about the anguish of my soul (Psalm 31:7).

When I am brokenhearted, the Lord is close to comfort me. When my spirit is crushed, He rescues me (Psalm 34:18).

God alone is my refuge, my safe place. I trust Him, for He is my God (Psalm 91:2).

When I am overwhelmed, I cry out to the Lord and plead for His mercy. I tell Him my troubles and share my complaints with Him. He alone knows the way I should go (Psalm 142:1-3).

Even during awful times, even as I grieve over my losses, I will still dare to hope (Lamentations 3:20).

God's mercy and love for me are constant, never-ending. His faithfulness is great and His mercy is new every morning (Lamentations 3:21-23).

When those around me are troubled, I give them the same comfort God has given me (2 Corinthians 1:4).

God renews my spirit day after day so, no matter what happens, I do not give up (2 Corinthians 4:16).

God provides for all my needs through His incredible riches given to me by Jesus (Philippians 4:19).

I give all my worries and cares to God because He deeply cares for me (1 Peter 5:7).

Lord, You are good. You are my mighty refuge when trouble comes. You care for me because I put my trust in You (Nahum 1:7).

I will give my burdens to the Lord and He will take care of me. I am His and He will not permit me to slip and fall (Matthew 11:28).

I have learned how to be content with whatever I have. I know how to live with almost nothing or with everything. I have learned the secret of living in every situation, whether it is with being full or hungry, with a lot of provisions or very little. Here is the secret: I can do everything through Christ, who gives me strength (Philippians 4:11-13).

Even when I walk through trouble, God will preserve my life (Psalm 138:7).

I will wait for You, Lord; I will be strong and take heart. I will wait for You, Lord (Psalm 27:14).

I trust in God's unfailing love. I rejoice because He rescues me. I sing praises to the Lord because He is good to me (Psalm 13:5-6).

The Lord gives me power when I am weary and increases my strength when I am weak (Isaiah 40:29).

I will be strong and take heart for I hope in the Lord (Psalm 31:24).

God has said, "I am the one who comforts you. So why do you fear mere humans?" (Isaiah 51:11).

Jesus has given me a gift—a deep peace of mind and heart. This is peace the world could never give me. So, now I do not need to be troubled or afraid (John 14:27).

Courage

Almighty God, You give me strength. You are my God. You save me. You are my Heavenly Father. I will praise and exalt You (Exodus 15:2).

I am full of courage, secure and confident because there is hope in You, my God. I find safety all around me and I rest in You (Job 11:18).

I will be strong and courageous! I won't be afraid or full of terror. I won't panic because You, the Lord my God, will personally go ahead of me! You will not fail! You will never abandon me (Deuteronomy 31:6).

I am strong and courageous, not afraid or discouraged, because God is with me wherever I go (Joshua 1:9).

I don't ever have to be afraid or discouraged. I can be strong, for the Lord is taking care of that which is against me, just like He did for Joshua and his men (Joshua 10:25).

The Lord is my strength; He will save me. I sing about it because I trust Him, and I will not be afraid. He will give me victory (Isaiah 12:2).

The Lord, who is holy and inhabits eternity, says that He will restore my crushed spirit when I humbly come to Him. When I am repentant, He will revive my heart with courage (Isaiah 57:15).

I hope and pray expectantly that I will never be ashamed of Christ but will remain bold for Him. I want my life to bring honor to Christ in my living and in my dying (Philippians 1:20).

Christ empowers me, so I can do everything through Him using the strength He gives me (Philippians 4:13).

Like Moses who left Egypt not fearing the King's anger because He trusted God, I need to keep doing right, keeping my eyes on the One who is invisible (Hebrews 11:27).

I can be strong and full of courage. I don't have to be afraid because the Lord God, my God, is with me. He will not abandon me or fail me (1 Chronicles 28:20).

I wait on the Lord and He renews my strength. He helps me soar like an eagle, run without getting weary, and walk without fainting (Isaiah 40:31).

I lie down and sleep because You alone, Lord, make me safe (Psalm 4:8).

Lord, I rejoice in You! I am blessed. I am full of joy and singing because I take refuge in you. You protect me with Your shield of love (Psalm 5:11-12).

I trust in God's unfailing love. I rejoice because He rescues me. I sing praises to the Lord because He is good to me (Psalm 13:5-6).

The Lord is my shield, the One who upholds my honor, who lifts my head from shame and discouragement (Psalm 3:3).

I love You, Lord, for You are my strength, rock, fortress, deliverer, refuge, and shield. You are the power that delivers me from my troubles. In Your presence, I find safety (Psalm 18:1-2).

God, You equip me with Your strength (Psalm 18:32).

The Lord God is my light and my salvation, the stronghold of my life. I will not be afraid (Psalm 27:1).

I know that my help comes from the Lord who made heaven and earth (Psalm 121:2).

God alone is my refuge, my safe place. I trust Him, for He is my God (Psalm 91:2).

When I am overwhelmed, I cry out to the Lord and plead for His mercy. I tell Him my troubles and share my complaints with Him. He alone knows the way I should go (Psalm 142:1-3).

I will not fear, for God is with me. He is my God. He will strengthen, help, and hold me up with His victorious right hand (Isaiah 41:10).

I am not anxious about my life—not what I will eat or wear, for God takes care of the smallest birds and, surely, He will take care of me (Luke 12:22-23).

I am more than a conqueror through Christ who loves me. I am convinced that nothing can ever separate me from the love of God. Not death or life, angels or demons, fears about today or all my worries about tomorrow. Not even hell itself can separate me from God's love. Nothing above the sky or in the earth below, nothing in all of creation will ever, ever be able to separate me from the love of God that was given to me through Christ Jesus (Romans 8:37-39).

With God's help, I will be on guard. I will stand firm in my faith, will be courageous and strong, and do everything with love (1 Corinthians 16:13-14).

God renews my spirit day after day so, no matter what happens, I do not give up (2 Corinthians 4:16).

I will be strong in the Lord and His almighty power. To stand strong against the tactics of Satan, I will put on all of God's armor. I am not fighting against ordinary enemies, but against wicked authorities, mighty powers and evil spirits in dark spiritual warfare. To win this battle, I will put on and use every piece of God's armor. This will help me resist the enemy. I will put on the belt of truth and armor, protecting my heart, which is God's righteousness. For shoes, I will wear the peace that comes from God's forgiveness. I will use the shield of faith to protect myself from the fiery arrows of the devil. I will wear the helmet of salvation and use the mighty Spirit's sword which is the Word of God (Ephesians 6:10-18).

When I pray, God's peace, which is way beyond my comprehension, calms my heart and eases my mind (Philippians 4:7).

I let my roots grow down deep into Christ and I build my life on Him. Therefore, my faith grows strong in the truth that I was taught, and I overflow with thankfulness (Colossians 2:7).

I won't let my heart get troubled, because I believe in God and His Son Jesus (John 14:1).

I have learned how to be content with whatever I have. I know how to live with almost nothing or with everything. I have learned the secret of living in every situation, whether it is with being full or hungry, with a lot of provisions or very little. Here is the secret: I can do everything through Christ, who gives me strength (Philippians 4:11-13).

The Lord will rescue me; He is my stronghold during troubles (Psalm 37:39).

I will wait for You, Lord; I will be strong and take heart. I will wait for You, Lord (Psalm 27:14).

When my heart is anxious, I will say to myself, "Be brave and do not fear, for God is coming with His mighty power to destroy all that comes against me. He will save me" (Isaiah 35:4).

Because I am a child of God and His servant, no weapon that comes against me will succeed. Every voice that is raised against me will be silenced. The Lord declares it (Isaiah 54:17).

Guidance

The Lord is my teacher. Even in adversity, I will see Him. When I don't know whether to go right or left, I will hear Him say, "This is the way you should go" (Isaiah 30:20-21).

For God is my God forever. He will be my guide to the end (Psalm 48:14).

With my mind, I can make plans, but it is God who directs my steps (Proverbs 16:9).

The Lord directs my steps and delights in every detail of my life (Psalm 37:23).

Lord, I am never out of Your awareness. I can never escape Your presence. If I go to heaven or hell, You are there. If I fly with rapid speed to the depth of the farthest ocean, even there I will have Your guidance and strength to help me (Psalm 119:7-10).

God, You show me the path of life. Your presence gives me great joy and I enjoy the pleasure of living with You forever (Psalm 16:11).

The Lord continually guides me. He gives my soul water when I am parched. He restores my strength. I am like a flourishing well-watered garden. I am like a stream that never stops flowing (Isaiah 58:11).

I will listen to the Holy Spirit because it is true. He will guide me into all truth. He won't speak on his own authority, but he hears from the Heavenly Father (John 16:13).

If I let the Holy Spirit guide my life, I won't be giving in to my human lust with its cravings (Galatians 5:16).

When I trust in the Lord with all my heart and quit depending on my own understanding, when I seek His will in all I do, He will show me what path to take (Proverbs 3:5-6).

Lord, You have redeemed me and lead me with your unfailing love. You guide me to Your sacred presence with Your might (Exodus 15:13).

I become wiser than even my enemies when I use Your Word as my continuous guide (Psalm 119:98).

I use Your Word as a lamp to help me see on my journey. It shows me where to go (Psalm 119:105).

Father God, please direct my path according to Your Word. I do not want sin to rule over me (Psalm 119:133).

Lord, guide me with Your light and truth. Let it lead me into Your Holy Presence (Psalm 43:3).

Lord, I will sing for joy with the whole world because You govern the world fairly and guide all the nations (Psalm 67:4).

The Lord teaches me about the way I should go. He watches over me and advises me on my journey (Psalm 32:8).

Even when I am spiritually blind, the Lord will lead me down a new path, He will guide me along an unfamiliar trail. He brightens the darkness and smooths out the road ahead of me. God will do this for me because He has not forsaken me (Isaiah 42:16).

Lord, I belong to You. You hold my hand and counsel me with Your guidance, ever leading me toward a wonderful destiny with You (Psalm 73:23-24).

Forgiveness/Salvation

The Lord is full of grace and compassion toward me. He is slow to anger and overflowing with love (Psalm 145:8).

Lord, help me to remember that You said if I forgive those who sin against me, that my Heavenly Father will forgive me, as well. But if I refuse to forgive others, my Heavenly Father will not forgive my sins. I know that I am saved by grace and not works, but this shows me how serious You are about forgiveness. Help me to follow Your example and be forgiving of others (Matthew 6:14,15).

The Lord is slow to anger and filled with unfailing love, forgiving every kind of sin and rebellion (Numbers 14:18).

I know that God is a God of forgiveness, gracious and merciful, slow to become angry, and rich in unfailing love. He will not abandon me (Nehemiah 9:17).

God has forgiven all my wrongdoing, He has dismissed all my sins (Psalm 85:2).

God is ready to settle it with me right now. Though my wrongdoing has stained me as red as scarlet, if I come to Him, He will make me clean like fresh white snow. Yes, as deep red as crimson, He will make me white as unblemished wool (Isaiah 1:19).

I praise God for the wondrous unlimited grace he has lavished upon me because I belong to Jesus, His dear Son. God is so rich in mercy and grace toward me that He purchased my freedom with the blood of his Son, Jesus. He has forgiven me for all of my wrongdoing (Ephesians 1:6-7).

I will forsake my wickedness and all my thoughts of wrongdoing. I will return to the Lord and He will have mercy on me. He will generously forgive me (Isaiah 55:7).

As far as the east is from the west, that is how far God has separated the penalty of my sin from me (Psalm 103:12).

God will cleanse me from all the guilt of my wrongdoing that I have done against Him. He will graciously forgive all my sins and my heinous rebellion against Him (Jeremiah 33:8).

God will forgive all my wickedness and won't remember any of my sins ever again (Hebrews 8:12).

When I sin, I have a Person defending me before God the Father—Jesus Christ, my Lord. He is my righteousness (1 John 2:1).

I am led by the Spirit of God; therefore, I am a child of God (Romans 8:14).

Because I am a child of God, I have the Spirit of Jesus in me crying out, "Dear Heavenly Father." I am no longer a servant, but a child of God and, if a true child, then I am really an heir of God through Christ (Galatians 4:6-7).

I have been saved because of God's tremendous mercy, not because of any good things I have done. God washed away my wrongdoing with the blood of Jesus, resulting in my new birth into His family. I have a new life now living with the Holy Spirit inside me. God has graciously given me the Holy Spirit because of all that Jesus Christ, my Savior, has done (Titus 3:5-6).

My spirit rejoices because of knowing God as my Savior (Luke 1:47).

Though I am overwhelmed by my sins, You forgive them all (Psalm 65:3).

God so loved me that He sacrificed His one and only Son so, when I chose to believe and receive this sacrifice, I was given eternal life instead of being condemned to perish forever (John 3:16).

I know that he (Jesus) really is the Savior of the world (John 4:42).

I know that Jesus came so He can seek out and save those that are lost (Luke 19:10).

For the honor of His name, the Lord forgives my many, many sins (Psalm 25:11).

My Lord is a God of compassion and mercy. He is slow to get angry and filled with unfailing love and faithfulness (Psalm 86:15).

Because Christ died for my wrongdoing and I have accepted His gift of forgiveness, I am no longer living under the cloud of condemnation (Romans 8:1).

I have a deep joy because my disobedience is forgiven, my sin has been put out of sight! Yes, I have joy because You have cleared me of guilt and I can live my life in complete honesty. I remember, when I did not confess my sins. I was deeply troubled—it affected my whole body. I was in deep despair all day long. Every day, Your hand was heavy upon me until I had no strength at all. Finally, I stopped hiding my guilt and confessed my sins to You. I told myself, I will trust God and confess all my wrongdoing to

Him. That's when You totally forgave me! All my guilt is gone (Psalm 32:1-5).

God's mercy and love for me are constant, never-ending. His faithfulness is great and His mercy is new every morning (Lamentations 3:21-23).

Thank God! Once I was a slave of sin, but now I obey His teaching with my whole heart (Romans 16:7).

The temptations in my life are no different from what others experience. God's faithfulness won't allow me to be tempted more than I can stand. He shows me a way out, so I can be victorious (1 Corinthians 10:13).

When I confess my sins to God, He is faithful and just to forgive me of all my sins and cleanse me from all my wrongdoing (1 John 1:9).

For it is through God's remarkable compassion and favor, His grace, that I have been delivered from judgment and given eternal life. It was nothing I have done. It is a gift from God, so I can't take any credit for it (Ephesians 2:8-9).

I know that as a child of God, I do not make a practice of sinning, for Jesus holds me securely, and in Christ, the evil one cannot touch me (1 John 5:18).

I am made right with God by placing my faith in Jesus Christ. This is the same for everyone who believes, no matter who we are. Why? Because all of us have sinned and have come up short against God's holy standard. However, God, because of His grace, has made me right in His sight. He can do this because Jesus Christ paid the penalty for my sins with His own blood (Romans 3:22-24).

I have been born again and saved for all of eternity because I recognize the power, authority, and majesty of Jesus as God, acknowledging and confessing to others that Jesus is Lord, believing that God the Father raised Him from the dead (Romans 10:9).

I know that God made the sinless Christ an offering for my sin so that I could be made right with God through Christ (2 Corinthians 5:21).

God loved me so much and was so merciful that even though I was guilty and lost because of my deliberate wrongdoing, He lavished His grace upon me and saved me, giving me a new clean life. This happened when He raised Christ from the dead (Ephesians 2:4-5).

God instructs me to say, "No" and to turn from godless living and sinful pleasures. Instead, I should live in this evil world with self-control, wisdom, righteousness, and devotion to God (Titus 2: 12).

I belong to Christ and am a new person. My old life is gone and now I am living a new life (2 Corinthians 5:17).

The Spirit of God anointed Jesus to bring me the good news. He was sent to bring comfort to my damaged emotions and set me free from any and all bondage in my life (Isaiah 61:1).

It was God's plan from before time to lavish His grace upon me through Christ Jesus, by not giving me what I deserve. Instead, He saved me and has called me to live a holy life honoring Him (2 Timothy 1:9).

Christ gave His life to free me from every kind of sin. He cleanses me, making me His very own, totally committed to doing good deeds (Titus 2:14).

Hope/Patience

When I am distressed, I can cry out to You, Lord. Yes, I can call upon You for help. You are my God and You will hear me. My cry will reach Your ears (2 Samuel 22:7).

I am convinced that the Lord is always with me, that is why I will not be shaken. Lord, You are right here with me (Psalm 16:8).

The joy of the Lord is my strength (Nehemiah 8:10).

The Lord will show me the right path and point out which way I should go. He will lead me with His truth and teach me, for He is the God who saves me. All day long I will put my hope in Him (Psalm 25:4-5).

I must keep my eyes on Jesus, the originator and finisher of my faith, who, because of the joy that would be the result of His crucifixion, endured all the pain, took all the shame and then rose again and is now at the right hand of God. I must remember all the hostility He suffered and endured, lest I become weary and discouraged with my own situation (Hebrews 12:2-3).

I trust in God and I meditate on His unfailing love for me each morning (Psalm 143:8).

God refreshes my soul and gives me strength. He guides me along the right path, bringing honor to His name (Psalm 23:3).

The Lord is my teacher. Even in adversity, I will see Him. When I don't know whether to go right or left, I will hear Him say, "This is the way you should go" (Isaiah 30:20-21).

Even when I stumble, Your words, Lord, uphold me. You strengthen my legs and keep me from falling (Job 4:4).

I will let the Lord teach me the way to live. He will lead me on the right path (Psalm 27:11).

Lord, please show me Your ways so I can understand and know You more fully and enjoy Your favor (Exodus 33:13).

For God is my God forever. He will be my guide to the end (Psalm 48:14).

I am blessing You, Lord, because You guide me. Even at night, You instruct my heart (Psalm 16:7).

When I trust in the Lord with all my heart and quit depending on my own understanding, when I seek His will in all I do, He will show me what path to take (Proverbs 3:5-6).

God guides me and teaches me the right way (Isaiah 28:26).

Even if I walk through the darkest valley, I will not fear, for You are right here with me. Your rod and staff comfort and protect me. You have prepared a feast for me in the presence of my enemies. You honor me, anointing my head with oil. Truly my cup overflows with blessings (Psalm 23:4-5).

The joy of the Lord is my strength (Nehemiah 8:10).

I am full of courage, secure and confident because there is hope in You, my God. I find safety all around me and I rest in You (Job 11:18).

I trust in God's unfailing love. I rejoice because He rescues me. I sing praises to the Lord because He is good to me (Psalm 13:5-6).

Lord, I am trusting You. You are my God and I know my future is in Your hands (Psalm 31:14-15).

I take great delight in the Lord and He gives me the desires of my heart (Psalm 37:4).

I praise God, the Father of our Lord Jesus Christ, who is my merciful Father and the source of all my comfort (2 Corinthians 1:3).

The Lord knows exactly what I long for. He hears every sigh I make (Psalm 38:9).

Even if my health fails and I grow weary, God will still be the strength of my heart. He is mine forever (Psalm 73:26).

When I need help, God hears my prayer and answers me (Psalm 86:11).

Your unfailing love and faithfulness cause me to say, "Not to me, O Lord, not to me, but to Your name goes all the glory" (Psalm 115:1).

All of God's plans for my life will work out because His faithful love endures forever (Psalm 138:8).

Even during awful times, even as I grieve over my losses, I will still dare to hope (Lamentations 3:20).

I bring my questions and concerns to the Lord and wait to see what He says and how He will answer me (Habakkuk 2:1).

Lord, when I am aware of Your unfailing love for me, I walk faithfully according to Your truth (Psalm 26:3).

I know that anything is possible if a person believes. So, I cry out, "I do believe! Help me with my unbelief" (Mark 9:22-24).

The temptations in my life are no different from what others experience. God's faithfulness won't allow me to be tempted more than I can stand. He shows me a way out, so I can be victorious (1 Corinthians 10:13).

I am empowered with inner strength through the Holy Spirit and God's glorious, unlimited resources (Ephesians 3:16).

I pray that my heart and mind might be open to experiencing more of God's incredible power in my life—the same mighty power that raised Jesus from the dead (Ephesians 1:17-20).

God has said, "I will never leave you or forsake you" (Hebrews 13:5).

Jesus said, "I am always with you, even to the end of the age" (Matthew 28:20).

Love for Others

If I am kind to the needy, I am really doing it to the Lord. He will reward me for what is done (Proverbs 19:17).

When I give a banquet, I need to invite the poor, the crippled, the broken, and the blind. Then I will be blessed (Luke 14:13).

I must help bear other people's burdens, thus fulfilling the law of Christ (Galatians 6:2).

If I despise my neighbor I am doing wrong, but I will be blessed if I am kind to those in need (Proverbs 14:21).

Christ gave us a new commandment that I must follow—love one another. As Christ has loved me, I must love others (John 13:34).

Since my soul has been purified of my sins when I obeyed the truth, I must have a sincere love for my brothers and sisters in Christ. I must love them deeply with all my heart (1 Peter 1:22).

I must not seek any revenge or bear a grudge. Instead, I am to love my neighbor as I love myself (Leviticus 19:18).

I must live a life that is filled with love like Christ who loved me and gave Himself a sacrifice for me, a fragrant offering to God (Ephesians 5:2).

I need to realize how much Jesus desires for me to help others as is evident when with sincerity and affection, Jesus told a rich young man, "You are lacking something. Sell everything you have and give it to the poor. This will transfer your riches to heaven. Then come and follow me" (Mark 10:21).

If Christ, who is my Lord and teacher, served His disciples by washing their feet, then I will follow that example and serve others (John 13:14-15).

Real greatness is becoming a servant to others. Being first is really being the slave of others. This is how Christ lived His life. He served others and gave up His life to be a sacrifice for all of mankind (Mark 10:43-45).

I want to be like the early church where they were united in heart and mind. They didn't claim anything to be their own but shared everything they had (Acts 4:32).

I do not want to be a hypocrite, ignoring the heavier things of justice, mercy, and faith (Matthew 23:23).

I rejoice in fully knowing that the Lord is God! He made me, and I am His. I am His, a sheep enjoying His pasture (Psalm 100:3).

I must think and live in humility like Christ who, even though He was God, humbled Himself and became human. As a human, He lived in humility even to the point of allowing Himself to be crucified as a sacrifice for all of mankind (Philippians 2:5-8).

If I am generous and share my food with those in need, I will be truly blessed (Proverbs 22:9).

I need wisdom from God that is pure, peaceable, gentle and willing to listen to others, full of compassion, mercy and the fruit of doing good (James 3:17).

I know what love is because Christ exemplified it by laying down His life for me. Therefore, I must lay down my life for others (1 John 3:16).

With all my material blessings, I need to make sure I am not arrogant or put my hope in them. Instead, I must put my confidence in God who has given me everything that I enjoy. I must do good for others and be generous, willing to share with those in need (1 Timothy 6:17-18).

I must continue to love others because love comes from God. Anyone who loves is a child of God and knows God. If I or anyone else does not love, then we really don't know God because God is love (1 John 4:7-8).

Since God loves me so much, I must, in turn, love others. I have never seen God, but if I love others, then God lives in me and His love is fully expressed through me (1 John 4:11-12).

This is what the Lord has commanded me to do—share my food with the hungry, provide shelter to those that need it, give clothes to those without, and do not forsake my own relatives (Isaiah 58:7).

Peace

I will be strong and courageous! I won't be afraid or full of terror. I won't panic because You, the Lord my God, will personally go ahead of me! You will not fail! You will never abandon me (Deuteronomy 31:6).

I am strong and courageous, not afraid or discouraged, because God is with me wherever I go (Joshua 1:9).

I will let the peace of God guide and direct my heart (Colossians 3:15).

I lie down and sleep because You alone, Lord, make me safe (Psalm 4:8).

In Christ, I have learned to be content with whatever I have (Philippians 4:11).

I love You, Lord, for You are my strength, rock, fortress, deliverer, refuge, and shield. You are the power that delivers me from my troubles. In your presence, I find safety (Psalm 18:1-2).

It is true that God's pursues me with His goodness and His unfailing love every day of my life (Psalm 23:6).

When I am brokenhearted, the Lord is close to comfort me. When my spirit is crushed, He rescues me (Psalm 34:18).

I trust in God and I meditate on His unfailing love for me each morning (Psalm 143:8).

I am filled with joy and peace because I am trusting in God (Romans 15:13).

When I pray, God's peace, which is way beyond my comprehension, calms my heart and eases my mind (Philippians 4:7).

God does not give me a spirit of fear. Instead, He gives me power, love, and self-control (2 Timothy 1:7).

I praise God, the Father of our Lord Jesus Christ, who is my merciful Father and the source of all my comfort (2 Corinthians 1:3).

God will keep me in perfect peace as my mind stays focused on Him and I trust in Him (Isaiah 26:3).

I will let the peace of God rule in my heart and be thankful (Colossians 3:15).

God provides for all my needs through His incredible riches given to me by Jesus (Philippians 4:19).

A wonderful attribute to have is to be godly while being content (1 Timothy 6:6).

Jesus has given me a gift—a deep peace of mind and heart. This is peace the world could never give me. So, now I do not need to be troubled or afraid (John 14:27).

I experience the Kingdom of God when I am living righteously with peace and joy in the Holy Spirit (Romans 14:17).

When I walk through a dark valley, I will choose not to be afraid. I can do this because You, O Lord, are close beside me. Like a shepherd, You protect me with your rod and staff and give me comfort (Psalm 23:4).

When I am spiritually minded, I experience life and peace (Romans 8:6).

I am convinced that nothing can ever separate me from God's love--not death nor life, angels nor demons, fears for today nor our worries about tomorrow. Not even the powers of hell can separate me from God's love. Not power above or below the earth— indeed, nothing in all creation will ever, ever be able to separate me from the love that God has for me revealed in Christ Jesus our Lord (Romans 8:38-39).

Self-Control Over
Addictions/Habits

Thank God! Once I was a slave of sin, but now I obey His teaching with my whole heart (Romans 16:7).

The Lord gives me strength and makes me want to sing His praise. He gives me victory! I hear songs of joy and victory sung by the godly. God's strong arm has done magnificent things (Psalm 118:14-15).

When I confess my sins to God, He is faithful and just to forgive me of all my sins and cleanse me from all my wrongdoing (1 John 1:9).

Christ's love controls me (2 Corinthians 5:14).

I will come to Jesus when I am weary and my burdens are heavy because I know he will give me rest (Matthew 11:28).

I must keep a close watch and ask God for help so that I will not give in to temptation. My spirit is willing, but alone I am weak (Matthew 26:41).

I know that as a child of God, I do not make a practice of sinning, for Jesus holds me securely, and in Christ, the Evil One cannot touch me (1 John 5:18).

The temptations in my life are no different from what others experience. God's faithfulness won't allow me to be tempted more than I can stand. He shows me a way out, so I can be victorious (1 Corinthians 10:13).

I belong to Christ and am a new person. My old life is gone and now I am living a new life (2 Corinthians 5:17).

I must beware! I don't want my heart to get depressed and hardened by partying and drunkenness, and by the anxieties of this life (Luke 21:34).

Because of all Christ has done for me, I will please God by giving my body and mind to Him. I will worship Him by being a holy living sacrifice (Romans 12:1).

I live as a citizen of heaven and conduct myself in a manner worthy of the Good News about Christ (Philippians 1:27).

It is time that I realize that my body is a temple of the Holy Spirit, who lives in me and was given to me by God Himself. I don't belong to myself. I am not my own boss—I was bought by God at the highest price imaginable, the death of His Son Jesus. Therefore, I must honor God with all that I am (1 Corinthians 6:19-20).

God does not give me a spirit of fear. Instead, He gives me power, love, and self-control (2 Timothy 1:7).

Jesus knows my weaknesses because He was tempted like me, but He did not sin. Therefore, I can receive His mercy and grace when I need it (Hebrews 4:15).

God has equipped me with all I need for doing His will. He will produce, through the power of Christ, every good thing that is pleasing to Him (Hebrews 13:21-22).

Lord, I have hidden Your Word in my heart so I won't sin against You (Psalm 119:11).

Father God, please direct my path according to Your Word. I do not want sin to rule over me (Psalm 119:133).

I won't participate in the darkness of wild parties, drunkenness, sexual wrongdoing, immoral living, or quarreling and jealousy. Instead, I will live in the conscious awareness of the presence of the Lord Jesus Christ. I will cease to think about ways to indulge my evil desires (Romans 13:13-14).

I want the Holy Spirit to produce His fruit in my life. The fruit is love, joy, peace, patience, kindness, goodness, faithfulness, gentleness and self-control (Galatians 5:22-23).

I belong to Christ; therefore, I will put to death my sinful passions and desires (Galatians 5:24).

Once I was full of darkness, but now I have the light of the Lord in me. So, I will live as a person of light, being careful to know what pleases the Lord and doing right. I will not participate in the worthless deeds of evil and darkness. Instead, I will expose them (Ephesians 5:8-11).

I will be careful how I live. I don't want to live like a fool—I want to live with wisdom. I will make the most of all the opportunities God has given me. I won't act thoughtlessly but will try to ascertain what the Lord wants me to do. I won't let substance take over my life because it will ruin it. Instead, I will seek to be filled with the Holy Spirit (Ephesians 5:15-18).

Christ empowers me, so I can do everything through Him using the strength He gives me (Philippians 4:13).

God instructs me to say, "No" and to turn from godless living and sinful pleasures. Instead, I should live in this evil world with self-control, wisdom, righteousness, and devotion to God (Titus 2: 12). I must prepare my mind for action and exercise self-control. Putting all my hope in my eternity with Jesus, I must live as an obedient child of God. I can't slip back into my old ways of living selfishly, satisfying my own desires. I didn't know any better then, but now I need to be holy in everything I do, just as God, who chose me to live for Him, is holy (1 Peter 1:13-15).

I will remain sober. I will be alert and cautious at all times. Satan, the enemy of my soul, is prowling around like a roaring lion ready to pounce on me and devour me. Therefore, I will be vigilant in resisting him and constantly exercise my faith in the all-powerful true and living God who loves me (1 Peter 5:8-9).

A wonderful attribute to have is to be godly while being content (1 Timothy 6:6).

If I love this world and the things it entices me with, I will end up loving the world more than God the Father. When I give into cravings for physical pleasure, cravings for everything I see, or ungodly pride in the thing I accomplish or possess, that pursuit is not from God. I will not love what the world says is important—I will love God (1 John 2:15-16).

Strength

I seek for You, Lord, and Your strength. I desperately seek Your face so I can be continuously in Your presence (1 Chronicles 16:11).

The joy of the Lord is my strength (Nehemiah 8:10).

David found strength in the Lord his God, and so can I (1 Samuel 30:6).

With Your strength, Lord, I can defeat an army. You are my God; with You, I can scale any wall (2 Samuel 22:30).

The Lord gives me strength and blesses me with peace (Psalm 29:11).

God, You equip me with Your strength (Psalm 18:32).

My heart cries out, "Don't abandon me, Lord! I get my strength from You. Come quickly and save me" (Psalm 22:19).

God Almighty is my strength and shield. I am trusting in Him with all of my heart. I am filled with joy because He helps me. I burst out with a joyful song. Halleluiah! God gives me, and all His people, strength (Psalm 28:7-8).

Lord, both riches and honor come from You because You rule over everything. It is with Your might and strength that You make people great and give strength (1 Chronicles 29:12).

God refreshes my soul and gives me strength. He guides me along the right path, bringing honor to His name (Psalm 23:3).

Lord, You will give me strength because Your eyes search the whole world and You know that I am fully committed to You (2 Chronicles 16:9).

When I stumble, Lord, Your words uphold me. You strengthen my legs and keep me from falling (Job 4:4).

Lord, I rejoice in You! I am blessed. I am full of joy and singing because I take refuge in you. You protect me with Your shield of love (Psalm 5:11-12).

Almighty God, You give me strength. You are my God. You save me. You are my Heavenly Father. I will praise and exalt You (Exodus 15:2).

Christ has given me the authority to trample on snakes and scorpions, and authority over all the power of the enemy. Nothing will harm me. God is my refuge and strength; He is always ready to help me in times of trouble. So, I will not fear (Psalm 46:1-2).

For God is my God forever. He will be my guide to the end (Psalm 48:14).

Lord, You are my fortress and my strength. I will wait for You to rescue me (Psalm 59:9).

I will give my burdens to the Lord and He will take care of me. I am His, and He will not permit me to slip and fall (Psalm 55:22).

I love You, Lord, for You are my strength, rock, fortress, deliverer, refuge, and shield. You are the power that delivers me from my troubles. In Your presence, I find safety (Psalm 18:1-2).

I must careful to obey every command that God gives me so that I may have strength (Deuteronomy 11:8).

Give me strength, O Lord, to defend my cause; help me against my enemies (Deuteronomy 33:7).

I want to know Christ and experience the mighty power that raised him from the dead (Philippians 3:10).

I pray that I will be strengthened with all Your glorious power, so I will have all the endurance and patience I need (Colossians 1:11).

I must love the Lord my God with all of my heart, all of my soul, and all of my strength (Deuteronomy 6:5).

I am the Lord's servant. He is sovereign, and He has only begun to show me His greatness and the strength of His hand toward me (Deuteronomy 3:24).

Jesus Christ and God the Father, who graciously gives me eternal love, comfort, and hope, comforts and strengthens me now in every good thing I do and say (2 Thessalonians 2:16-17).

Jesus knows my weaknesses because He was tempted like me, but He did not sin. Therefore, I can receive His mercy and grace when I need it (Hebrews 4:15).

God has equipped me with all I need for doing His will. He will produce, through the power of Christ, every good thing that is pleasing to Him (Hebrews 13:21-22).

I want the Holy Spirit to produce His fruit in my life. The fruit is love, joy, peace, patience, kindness, goodness, faithfulness, gentleness and self-control (Galatians 5:22-23).

Christ empowers me, so I can do everything through Him using the strength He gives me (Philippians 4:13).

The Lord gives me power when I am weary and increases my strength when I am weak (Isaiah 40:29).

I will be strong and courageous! I won't be afraid or full of terror. I won't panic because You, the Lord my God, will personally go ahead of me! You will not fail! You will never abandon me (Deuteronomy 31:6).

Almighty God, You give me strength. You are my God. You save me. You are my Heavenly Father. I will praise and exalt You (Exodus 15:2).

I am full of courage, secure and confident because there is hope in You, my God. I find safety all around me and I rest in You (Job 11:18).

When doubts and anxiety fill my thoughts, Your comfort, God, renews my hope and I return to joy (Psalm 94:19).

If I commit my actions to the Lord and respond to His will and guidance, my plans will succeed (Proverbs 16:3).

I trust in God's unfailing love. I rejoice because He rescues me. I sing praises to the Lord because He is good to me (Psalm 13:5-6).

I lie down and sleep because You alone, Lord, make me safe (Psalm 4:8).

I will not conform to the secular worldview or mindset, but instead, I will let my mind be transformed by God as He renews my mind (Romans 12:2).

I will come to Jesus when I am weary and my burdens are heavy because I know he will give me rest (Matthew 11:28).

Jesus has given me a gift—a deep peace of mind and heart. This is peace the world could never give me. So, now I do not need to be troubled or afraid (John 14:27).

Trust

I seek for You, Lord, and Your strength. I desperately seek Your face so I can be continuously in Your presence (1 Chronicles 16:11).

I am full of courage, secure and confident because there is hope in You, my God. I find safety all around me and I rest in You (Job 11:18).

I lie down and sleep because You alone, Lord, make me safe (Psalm 4:8).

When I am living righteously, I do not fear bad news. Instead, I have a confident trust that God will take care of me. My heart is unwavering and fearless. I can triumphantly face what comes against me (Psalm 112:6-7).

Lord, I rejoice in You! I am blessed. I am full of joy and singing because I take refuge in you. You protect me with Your shield of love (Psalm 5:11-12).

The faith that I desire is being confident that I will get what I hope for. It is the conviction that what I can't see will come into being (Hebrews 11:1).

I trust in God's unfailing love. I rejoice because He rescues me. I sing praises to the Lord because He is good to me (Psalm 13:5-6).

The Lord is like a father to me, tender and compassionate (Psalm 103:13).

All of God's plans for my life will work out because His faithful love endures forever (Psalm 138:8).

I trust in God and I meditate on His unfailing love for me each morning (Psalm 143:8).

I know that anything is possible if a person believes. So, I cry out, "I do believe! Help me with my unbelief" (Mark 9:22-24).

I am not anxious about my life—not what I will eat or wear, for God takes care of the smallest birds and, surely, He will take care of me (Luke 12:22-23).

O Lord, I will pray to You. Please hear and be attentive to my groaning, O my King, my God. Please hear my cry for help! I pray only to You. Lord, hear my voice each morning, as I lay out my requests before You and wait expectantly (Psalm 5:1-3).

Even when I walk through trouble, God will preserve my life (Psalm 138:7).

Lord, You are good—a refuge in times of trouble. You care for me because I trust in You (Psalm 37:24).

Christ empowers me, so I can do everything through Him using the strength He gives me (Philippians 4:13).

The Lord will rescue me; He is my stronghold during troubles (Psalm 37:39).

I will wait for You, Lord; I will be strong and take heart. I will wait for You, Lord (Psalm 27:14).

WHEN I AM STRUGGLING WITH...

Anger
Depression
Discouragement
Distress
Doubt
Fear
Living the Christian Life
Loneliness
Lust
Stress
Temptations
Troubles
Worries

Anger

I take great delight in the Lord, and He gives me the desires of my heart (Psalm 37:4).

I must refrain from anger and turn away from being hateful. I need to stop fretting—it only leads to evil (Psalm 37:8).

When I am easily angered, I do foolish things (Proverbs 14:17).

When I give a kind answer, it keeps anger from erupting. A harsh response only gets others angry (Proverbs 15:1).

My temper only stirs up opposition, but when I am patient I can calm a quarrel (Proverbs 15:18).

It is better for me to be patient than simply be a warrior. It is better for me to control my temper than to be one who overtakes a city (Proverbs 16:32).

If I use wisdom, I will have patience and I will glorify God when I overlook an offense toward me (Proverbs 19:11).

When I act in anger, I stir up dissension. When I let my temper go, I commit many sins (Proverbs 29:22).

I need to be careful not to be quickly angered in my spirit, for anger is the way of fools (Ecclesiastes 7:9).

The temptations in my life are no different from what others experience. God's faithfulness won't allow me to be tempted more than I can stand. He shows me a way out, so I can be victorious (1 Corinthians 10:13).

When I get enraged, I need to be careful and not sin! I shouldn't end the day still being angry (Ephesians 4:26).

I must get rid of all bitterness, rage and anger, fighting and slander, and every form of hatred. Instead, I will be kind, compassionate to others, forgiving people in the same way Christ has forgiven me (Ephesians 4:31-32).

So, now I must get rid of anger, rage, hatred, slander and offensive language (Colossians 3:8).

I must be quick to listen, slow to speak out, and slow to become angry. My anger does not result in the righteous behavior that God desires of me (James 1:19-20).

God tells me not to take revenge but, instead, leave it up to God to get revenge. It is written, "It is mine to avenge, I will repay," says the Lord (Romans 12: 19).

If my enemy is hungry, I will feed him; if he is thirsty I will give him something to drink. This will be like heaping hot coals on their head. I will not be overcome with evil but will overcome evil with good (Romans 12:20-21).

I will humble myself before God so that at the proper time, He may exalt me (1 Peter 5:6).

Depression

Your presence, Lord, will go with me and give me rest (Exodus 33:14).

I will not be afraid or discouraged because the Lord Himself goes before me. He is with me and will never leave me or forsake me (Deuteronomy 3:18).

I am strong and courageous, not afraid or discouraged, because God is with me wherever I go (Joshua 1:9).

When I am distressed, I can cry out to You, Lord. Yes, I can call upon You for help. You are my God and You will hear me. My cry will reach Your ears (2 Samuel 22:7).

The joy of the Lord is my strength (Nehemiah 8:10).

I am full of courage, secure and confident because there is hope in You, my God. I find safety all around me and I rest in You (Job 11:18).

It is my desire that what I say and what I meditate on in my heart will be pleasing to God, my Rock and Redeemer (Psalm 19:14).

Lord, in my heart I have heard You say, "Come, talk with me." My heart shouts, "Yes, Lord, I am coming!" (Psalm 27:8).

I rejoice in God's unfailing love, for He sees my troubles and cares about the anguish of my soul (Psalm 31:7).

I will brag about the Lord. Let all who feel helpless take heart (Psalm 34:2).

When I am brokenhearted, the Lord is close to comfort me. When my spirit is crushed, He rescues me (Psalm 34:18).

I patiently waited for help from the Lord. He heard my cry, turned toward me, and lifted me out of my despair (Psalm 40:1-2).

I trust in God and I meditate on His unfailing love for me each morning (Psalm 143:8).

When I go through deep waters, God is with me. Through rivers of difficulty, I will not drown. Through fire of oppression I will not be burned up (Isaiah 43:2).

God renews my spirit day after day so, no matter what happens, I do not give up (2 Corinthians 4:16).

I will focus on this day. Forgetting the past, I look forward to what God has in store for me (Philippians 3:13).

I give all my worries and cares to God because He deeply cares for me (1 Peter 5:7).

I can come to God because heals those that are brokenhearted, and He heals their wounds (Psalm 147:3).

I will give my burdens to the Lord and He will take care of me. I am His, and He will not permit me to slip and fall (Psalm 55:22).

The Lord gives me power when I am weary and increases my strength when I am weak (Isaiah 40:29).

I am convinced that nothing can ever separate me from God's love--not death nor life, angels nor demons, fears for today nor our worries about tomorrow. Not even the powers of hell can separate me from God's love. Not power above or below the earth—indeed, nothing in all creation will ever, ever be able to separate me from the love that God has for me revealed in Christ Jesus our Lord (Romans 8:38-39).

Discouragement

I will not be afraid or discouraged because the Lord Himself goes before me. He is with me and will never leave me or forsake me (Deuteronomy 3:18).

I will be strong in the Lord and His almighty power. To stand strong against the tactics of Satan, I will put on all of God's armor. I am not fighting against ordinary enemies, but against wicked authorities, mighty powers and evil spirits in dark spiritual warfare. To win this battle, I will put on and use every piece of God's armor. This will help me resist the enemy. I will put on the belt of truth and armor, protecting my heart, which is God's righteousness. For shoes, I will wear the peace that comes from God's forgiveness. I will use the shield of faith to protect myself from the fiery arrows of the devil. I will wear the helmet of salvation and use the mighty Spirit's sword which is the Word of God (Ephesians 6:10-18).

I will be strong and courageous! I won't be afraid or full of terror. I won't panic because You, the Lord my God, will personally go ahead of me! You will not fail! You will never abandon me (Deuteronomy 31:6).

I will come to Jesus when I am weary and my burdens are heavy because I know He will give me rest (Matthew 11:28).

I am strong and courageous, not afraid or discouraged, because God is with me wherever I go (Joshua 1:9).

The Lord gives me power when I am weary and increases my strength when I am weak (Isaiah 40:29).

In all things pertaining to me, God is at work for the good (Romans 8:28).

When I am distressed, I can cry out to You, Lord. Yes, I can call upon You for help. You are my God and You will hear me. My cry will reach Your ears (2 Samuel 22:7).

I know that my help comes from the Lord who made heaven and earth (Psalm 121:2).

I am full of courage, secure and confident because there is hope in You, my God. I find safety all around me and I rest in You (Job 11:18).

It is true that God's pursues me with His goodness and His unfailing love every day of my life (Psalm 23:6).

I rejoice in God's unfailing love, for He sees my troubles and cares about the anguish of my soul (Psalm 31:7).

When I am overwhelmed, I cry out to the Lord and plead for His mercy. I tell Him my troubles and share my complaints with Him. He alone knows the way I should go (Psalm 142:1-3).

I must refrain from anger and turn away from being hateful. I need to stop fretting—it only leads to evil (Psalm 37:8).

I bring my questions and concerns to the Lord and wait to see what He says and how He will answer me (Habakkuk 2:1).

God renews my spirit day after day so, no matter what happens, I do not give up (2 Corinthians 4:16).

But God, who encourages those who are discouraged, encourages me (2 Corinthians 7:6).

When I pray, God's peace, which is way beyond my comprehension, calms my heart and eases my mind (Philippians 4:7).

I give all my worries and cares to God because He deeply cares for me (1 Peter 5:7).

I can come to God because heals those that are brokenhearted, and He heals their wounds (Psalm 147:3).

When I am overwhelmed, I cry out to the Lord; I plead for the Lord's mercy. I pour out my complaints before Him and tell Him all my troubles. He alone knows the way I should turn (Psalm 142:1-3).

I will give my burdens to the Lord and He will take care of me. I am His, and He will not permit me to slip and fall (Psalm 55:22).

I will be strong and take heart, for I hope in the Lord (Psalm 31:24).

Distress

I will not be afraid or discouraged because the Lord Himself goes before me. He is with me and will never leave me or forsake me (Deuteronomy 3:18).

When I am distressed, I can cry out to You, Lord. Yes, I can call upon You for help. You are my God and You will hear me. My cry will reach Your ears (2 Samuel 22:7).

In all things pertaining to me, God is at work for the good (Romans 8:28).

Even if I walk through the darkest valley, I will not fear, for You are right here with me. Your rod and staff comfort and protect me. You have prepared a feast for me in the presence of my enemies. You honor me, anointing my head with oil. Truly my cup overflows with blessings (Psalm 23:4-5).

Even when I stumble, Your words, Lord, uphold me. You strengthen my legs and keep me from falling (Job 4:4).

I am full of courage, secure and confident because there is hope in You, my God. I find safety all around me and I rest in You (Job 11:18).

I lie down and sleep because You alone, Lord, make me safe (Psalm 4:8).

Lord, I rejoice in You! I am blessed. I am full of joy and singing because I take refuge in you. You protect me with Your shield of love (Psalm 5:11-12).

I trust in God's unfailing love. I rejoice because He rescues me. I sing praises to the Lord because He is good to me (Psalm 13:5-6).

When I am brokenhearted, the Lord is close to comfort me. When my spirit is crushed, He rescues me (Psalm 34:18).

I patiently waited for help from the Lord. He heard my cry, turned toward me and lifted me out of my despair (Psalm 40:1-2).

I know that my help comes from the Lord who made heaven and earth (Psalm 121:2).

Even if my health fails and I grow weary, God will still be the strength of my heart. He is mine forever (Psalm 73:26).

When I need help, God hears my prayer and answers me (Psalm 86:1).

God alone is my refuge, my safe place. I trust Him, for He is my God (Psalm 91:2).

When I am overwhelmed, I cry out to the Lord and plead for His mercy. I tell Him my troubles and share my complaints with Him. He alone knows the way I should go (Psalm 142:1-3).

I will not fear, for God is with me. He is my God. He will strengthen, help, and hold me up with His victorious right hand (Isaiah 41:10).

Even during awful times, even as I grieve over my losses, I will still dare to hope (Lamentations 3:20).

I know that anything is possible if a person believes. So, I cry out, "I do believe! Help me with my unbelief" (Mark 9:22-24).

God renews my spirit day after day so, no matter what happens, I do not give up (2 Corinthians 4:16).

I'm not anxious. Instead, I pray to God and, with thanksgiving, give Him all my requests (Philippians 4:6).

God provides for all my needs through His incredible riches given to me by Jesus (Philippians 4:19).

I give all my worries and cares to God because He deeply cares for me (1 Peter 5:7).

When I am overwhelmed, I cry out to the Lord and plead for His mercy. I tell Him my troubles and share my complaints with Him. He alone knows the way I should go (Psalm 142:1-3).

I give all my worries and cares to God because He deeply cares for me (1 Peter 5:7).

Lord, You are good. You are my mighty refuge when trouble comes. You care for me because I put my trust in You (Nahum 1:7).

I will come to Jesus when I am weary and my burdens are heavy because I know He will give me rest (Matthew 11:28).

God, who encourages those who are discouraged, encourages me (2 Corinthians 7:6).

The Lord gives me power when I am weary and increases my strength when I am weak (Isaiah 40:29).

I will be strong and take heart for I hope in the Lord (Psalm 31:24).

The Lord God takes hold of my hand and tells me, "Do not fear—I will help you" (Isaiah 41:13).

I can be pressured in every way but won't be crushed; I can be perplexed but won't be driven to despair. I could even be hunted down and persecuted, but I will not be deserted by God. I may be struck down, but I will never be destroyed (2 Corinthians 4: 8,9).

I rejoice in God's unfailing love, for He sees my troubles and cares about the anguish of my soul (Psalm 31:7).

I can say confidently that the Lord is my helper. I will not be afraid of what man can do to me (Hebrew 13:6).

Jesus has given me a gift—a deep peace of mind and heart. This is peace the world could never give me. So, now I do not need to be troubled or afraid (John 14:27).

I am convinced that nothing can ever separate me from God's love—not death nor life, angels nor demons, fears for today nor our worries about tomorrow. Not even the powers of hell can separate me from God's love. Not power above or below the earth—indeed, nothing in all creation will ever, ever be able to separate me from the love that God has for me revealed in Christ Jesus our Lord (Romans 8:38-39).

Doubt

Lord, I rejoice in You! I am blessed. I am full of joy and singing because I take refuge in you. You protect me with Your shield of love (Psalm 5:11-12).

It is my desire that what I say and what I meditate on in my heart will be pleasing to God, my Rock and Redeemer (Psalm 19:14).

It is true that God's pursues me with His goodness and His unfailing love every day of my life (Psalm 23:6).

When I trust in the Lord with all my heart and quit depending on my own understanding, when I seek His will in all I do, He will show me what path to take (Proverbs 3:5-6).

The Lord directs my steps and delights in every detail of my life (Psalm 37:23).

In all things pertaining to me, God is at work for the good (Romans 8:28).

When I come to God with reverence and I trust in Him, He will be my help and shield (Psalm 115:11).

The Lord listens to me when I cry out to Him and gives me the discerning mind that He promised to give me (Psalm 119:169).

God will keep me in perfect peace as my mind stays focused on Him and I trust in Him (Isaiah 26:3).

I am blessed as I trust in God and put my confidence and hope in Him (Jeremiah 17:7).

I have no fear because I realize that the Lord God is on my side. Therefore, what can any person really do to me? (Psalm 118:6).

God's mercy and love for me are constant, never-ending. His faithfulness is great and His mercy is new every morning (Lamentations 3:21-23).

When doubts and anxiety fill my thoughts, Your comfort, God, renews my hope and I return to joy (Psalm 94:19).

When I commit everything to the Lord and trust Him, He helps me (Psalm37:5).

I bring my questions and concerns to the Lord and wait to see what He says and how He will answer me (Habakkuk 2:1).

When I trust in the Lord, I become surrounded by His unfailing love (Psalm 32:10).

The faith that I desire is being confident that I will get what I hope for. It is the conviction that what I can't see will come into being (Hebrews 11:1).

I am convinced that nothing can ever separate me from God's love (Romans 8:38).

I give all my worries and cares to God because He deeply cares for me (1 Peter 5:7).

I will give my burdens to the Lord and He will take care of me. I am His, and He will not permit me to slip and fall (Psalm 55:22).

The Lord God takes hold of my hand and tells me, "Do not fear, I will help you" (Isaiah 41:13).

I do not have to be afraid of God, for I have received God's Spirit. He has made me His child and I now affectionately call him, "Daddy, Father." God's Spirit joins with my spirit, assuring me that I am His child (Romans 8:15-16).

I am convinced that nothing can ever separate me from God's love--not death nor life, angels nor demons, fears for today nor our worries about tomorrow. Not even the powers of hell can separate me from God's love. Not power above or below the earth— indeed, nothing in all creation will ever, ever be able to separate me from the love that God has for me revealed in Christ Jesus our Lord (Romans 8:38-39).

Fear/Anxiety

I will be strong and courageous! I won't be afraid or full of terror. I won't panic because You, the Lord my God, will personally go ahead of me! You will not fail! You will never abandon me (Deuteronomy 31:6).

I am strong and courageous, not afraid or discouraged, because God is with me wherever I go (Joshua 1:9).

When doubts and anxiety fill my thoughts, Your comfort, God, renews my hope and I return to joy (Psalm 94:19).

When I use common sense and discernment in my life, I can go to bed and sleep well without fear (Proverbs 3:21,24).

I listen to the Lord, so I end up living in peace, not in fear of any harm (Proverbs 1:33).

I cannot stop shaking. My fear and trembling overwhelm me. However, I will call upon God and He will rescue me (Psalm 55:5,16).

When my heart is anxious, I will say to myself, "Be brave and do not fear, for God is coming with His mighty power to destroy all that comes against me. He will save me" (Isaiah 35:4).

Anxiety weighs heavy on my heart, but encouragement makes me glad (Proverbs 12:25).

All my fretting and worry cannot add a single second to my life. Therefore, I will quit worrying about everything else (Luke 12:25-26).

I lie down and sleep because You alone, Lord, make me safe (Psalm 4:8).

I won't worry about tomorrow, for tomorrow will have enough worries of its own. I will trust You with the troubles I have today (Matthew 6:34).

I won't let my heart get troubled, because I believe in God and His Son Jesus (John 14:1).

I can be pressured in every way, but won't be crushed. I can be perplexed, but won't be driven to despair. I could even be hunted down and persecuted, but I will not be deserted by God. I may be struck down, but I will never be destroyed (2 Corinthians 4: 8-9).

I will not fear, for God is with me. He is my God. He will strengthen, help, and hold me up with His victorious right hand (Isaiah 41:10).

When I go through deep waters, God is with me. Through rivers of difficulty, I will not drown. Through the fires of oppression, I will not be burned up. For the Lord God, the Holy One will save me (Isaiah 43:1-3).

When I call, the Lord comes near and says, "Do not fear" (Lamentations 3:57).

I'm not anxious. Instead, I pray to God and, with thanksgiving, give Him all my requests (Philippians 4:6).

God provides for all my needs through His incredible riches, given to me by Jesus (Philippians 4:19).

God does not give me a spirit of fear. Instead, He gives me power, love, and self-control (2 Timothy 1:7).

I am more than a conqueror through Christ who loves me. I am convinced that nothing can ever separate me from the love of God. Not death or life, angels or demons, fears about today or all my worries about tomorrow. Not even hell itself can separate me from God's love. Nothing above the sky or in the earth below, nothing in all of creation will ever, ever be able to separate me from the love of God that was given to me through Christ Jesus (Romans 8:37-39).

I give all my worries and cares to God because He deeply cares for me (1 Peter 5:7).

With God's love, I have no fear because perfect love casts out all fear (1 John 4:18).

When I seek the Lord, He will answer me and deliver me from all my fears (Psalm 34:4).

God will keep me in perfect peace as my mind stays focused on Him and I trust in Him (Isaiah 26:3).

God has said, "I will never leave you or forsake you" (Hebrews 13:5).

Jesus said, "I am always with you, even to the end of the age" (Matthew 28:20).

Christ has given me the authority to trample on snakes and scorpions, and authority over all the power of the enemy. Nothing will harm me. God is my refuge and strength; He is always ready to help me in times of trouble. So, I will not fear (Psalm 46:1-2).

I will give my burdens to the Lord and He will take care of me. I am His, and He will not permit me to slip and fall (Psalm 55:22).

I will be strong and take heart, for I hope in the Lord (Psalm 31:24).

The Lord God takes hold of my hand and tells me, "Do not fear, I will help you" (Isaiah 41:13).

I can say confidently that the Lord is my helper. I will not be afraid of what man can do to me (Hebrew 13:6).

Jesus has given me a gift—a deep peace of mind and heart. This is peace the world could never give me. So, now I do not need to be troubled or afraid (John 14:27). I will place myself under God's protection. I will stay with Almighty God. I will confess that God alone is my refuge, my safe place. I trust Him, for He is my God (Psalm 91:1-2).

When I walk through a dark valley, I will choose not to be afraid. I can do this because You, O Lord, are close beside me. Like a shepherd, You protect me with Your rod and staff and give me comfort (Psalm 23:4).

I'm not anxious. Instead, I pray to God and, with thanksgiving, give Him all my requests (Philippians 4:6).

When I pray, God's peace, which is way beyond my comprehension, calms my heart and eases my mind (Philippians 4:7).

It is true that God's pursues me with His goodness and His unfailing love every day of my life (Psalm 23:6).

The Lord directs my steps and delights in every detail of my life (Psalm 37:23).

I praise God, the Father of our Lord Jesus Christ, who is my merciful Father and the source of all my comfort (2 Corinthians 1:3).

The Lord listens to me when I cry out to Him and gives me the discerning mind that He promised to give me (Psalm 119:169).

I am not anxious about my life—not what I will eat or wear, for God takes care of the smallest birds and, surely, He will take care of me (Luke 12:22-23).

I am empowered with inner strength through the Holy Spirit and God's glorious, unlimited resources (Ephesians 3:16).

I give all my worries and cares to God because He deeply cares for me (1 Peter 5:7).

When I am overwhelmed, I cry out to the Lord and plead for His mercy. I tell Him my troubles and share my complaints with Him. He alone knows the way I should go (Psalm 142:1-3).

I want the Holy Spirit to produce His fruit in my life. The fruit is love, joy, peace, patience, kindness, goodness, faithfulness, gentleness and self-control (Galatians 5:22-23).

A wonderful attribute to have is to be godly while being content (1 Timothy 6:6).

When I walk through a dark valley, I will choose not to be afraid. I can do this because You, O Lord, are close beside me. Like a shepherd, You protect me with your rod and staff and give me comfort (Psalm 23:4).

Living the Christian Life

Because of all that Christ has done for me, I will please God by giving my body and mind to Him. I will worship Him by being a holy living sacrifice. I will not conform to the secular worldview or mindset but, instead, I will let my mind be transformed by God as He renews my mind (Romans 12:1-2).

God has put Christ in the place of highest honor and has given Him a name above all other names. It is at the name of Jesus that I and everyone else that ever lived in heaven and on earth and under the earth will bow our knees before Him. All will proclaim that Jesus Christ is Lord of Lords! This will bring glory to God the Father (Philippians 2:9-11).

It is time that I realize that my body is a temple of the Holy Spirit, who lives in me and was given to me by God Himself. I don't belong to myself. I am not my own boss—I was bought by God at the highest price imaginable, the death of His Son Jesus. Therefore, I must honor God with all that I am (1 Corinthians 6:19-20).

Jesus is the vine and I am a branch. If I stay grafted into Him, I can't help but produce godly fruit in my life. I can never do that on my own (John 15: 5).

I do not have to be afraid of God, for I have received God's Spirit. He has made me His child and I now affectionately call him, "Daddy, Father." God's Spirit joins with my spirit, assuring me that I am His child (Romans 8:15-16).

If I say I am fellowshipping with Christ and living in evil darkness, I am lying. But if I resist the darkness and live in the light, just like Christ did, I will have fellowship with Him and His blood will cleanse me of all my evil (1 John 1:5-7).

Jesus stood at the door of my heart and knocked. I heard His voice, opened the door, and let Him in. He has come in and we are having great fellowship together (Revelation 3:20).

I am alive to live for and honor the Lord. If I die, that, too, will honor the Lord. So, whether I live or die, I belong to Him to bring Him honor (Romans 14:8).

I will love the Lord my God with all of my heart, all of my soul and all of my mind. I will love Him with all my might (Mark 12:30).

I must continue to love others because love comes from God. Anyone who loves is a child of God and knows God. If I or anyone else does not love, then we really don't know God, because God is love (1 John 4:7-8).

Christ dwells in my heart through faith. I am rooted and established in His love. And even though it is too great to fully understand, I strive to know how wide, long, deep and high the love of Christ really is so I can be full of the life and power that comes from experiencing that love (Ephesians 3:17-19).

As His disciple, I glorify my Heavenly Father when I produce godly fruit in my life (John 15:8).

I pray that my love may grow more and more, both in experiential knowledge and understanding (Philippians 1:9).

I thank God that my faith is growing more and more and that my love for my Christian brothers and sisters is increasing (1 Thessalonians 1:9).

I am filled with the fruit that comes from living righteously because of knowing Jesus. May God be glorified (Philippians 1:11).

I must prepare my mind for action and exercise self-control. Putting all my hope in my eternity with Jesus, I must live as an obedient child of God. I can't slip back into my old ways of living selfishly, satisfying my own desires. I didn't know any better then, but now I need to be holy in everything I do, just as God, who chose me to live for Him, is holy (1 Peter 1:13-15).

Because Christ has made it possible for me to experience the presence of God, I am being transformed more and more like Him. This is through the working of the Holy Spirit in my life (2 Corinthians 3:18).

I rejoice in fully knowing that the Lord is God! He made me, and I am His. I am His, a sheep enjoying His pasture (Psalm 100:3).

All of God's plans for my life will work out because His faithful love endures forever (Psalm 138:8).

I press on toward my goal of winning the heavenly prize that God has called me to win for His glory in Christ Jesus (Philippians 3:14).

I receive more and more grace and peace from God as I grow in my knowledge of Him and Jesus my Lord (2 Peter 1:2).

God, through His divine power, has given me everything I need for living a godly life (2 Peter 1:3).

God has given me precious promises that enable me to share His divine nature, escaping the trap of living worldly and following my own human lusts and desires (2 Peter 1:4).

Because of His grace and promises, I will make every effort to add to my faith, moral excellence, knowledge, self-control, patience, godliness, brotherly affection and love for everyone (2 Peter 1:5-7).

I am growing in the grace and knowledge of our Lord and Savior Jesus Christ (2 Peter 3:18).

Loneliness

Lord, in my heart I have heard You say, "Come, talk with me." My heart shouts, "Yes, Lord, I am coming!" (Psalm 27:8).

God has said, "I will never leave you or forsake you" (Hebrews 13:5).

Jesus said, "I am always with you, even to the end of the age" (Matthew 28:20).

The Lord will not abandon me because it will bring Him dishonor. It goes against who He is. It has pleased God to make me His own (1 Samuel 12:22).

I am living, and the Lord chooses to be with me. He is my mighty Savior who takes delight in me. He is glad to be with me. I rest in His love for He calms all my fears. He rejoices over me with joyful songs and celebration (Zephaniah 3:17).

I will not fear, for God is with me. He is my God. He will strengthen, help, and hold me up with His victorious right hand (Isaiah 41:10).

The Lord God takes hold of my hand and tells me, "Do not fear, I will help you" (Isaiah 41:13).

The Lord is the Father to the fatherless, the protector of widows. He is the God who dwells in holiness. He makes a home for the lonely, He set the prisoners free and makes them prosper giving them joy (Psalm 68:5-6).

Lord, please turn Your head toward me and have mercy on me. I am alone and in deep distress (Psalm 25:16).

I am looking for someone to help me, but no one is paying attention to me. No one cares about what happens to me. However, I cry out to You, O Lord, and You become my refuge, everything I want in life (Psalm 142:4-5).

If my father and mother abandon me, the Lord will take me in (Psalm 27:10).

I will be strong and courageous! I won't be afraid or full of terror. I won't panic because You, the Lord my God, will personally go ahead of me! You will not fail! You will never abandon me (Deuteronomy 31:6).

I am strong and courageous, not afraid or discouraged, because God is with me wherever I go (Joshua 1:9).

I am convinced that the Lord is always with me, that is why I will not be shaken. Lord, You are right here with me (Psalm 16:8).

I am not alone, for the Father is with me (John 16:32).

I need to be like the early church, joining other believers in devoting myself to solid Bible teaching, fellowshipping with other believers and praying for each other (Acts2:42).

I give all my worries and cares to God because He deeply cares for me (1 Peter 5:7).

When I am with other believers, I want to encourage them in their faith and allow them to encourage me (Romans 1:12).

I want to be like Abraham. He believed and put his faith in what God said. This faith was seen by God as righteous and God called him His friend (James 2:23).

God is with me even when I am walking through the darkest trials of my life. Therefore, I will not fear, for I am never alone. Like a loving shepherd with His tender sheep, His rod and staff protect me and bring me comfort (Psalm 23:4).

I am convinced that nothing can ever separate me from God's love--not death nor life, angels nor demons, fears for today nor our worries about tomorrow. Not even the powers of hell can separate me from God's love. Not power above or below the earth— indeed, nothing in all creation will ever, ever be able to separate me from the love that God has for me revealed in Christ Jesus our Lord (Romans 8:38-39).

Lust

If I love this world and the things it entices me with, I will end up loving the world more than God the Father. When I give into cravings for physical pleasure, cravings for everything I see, or ungodly pride in the thing I accomplish or possess, that pursuit is not from God. I will not love what the world says is important—I will love God (1 John 2:15-16).

I will not conform to the secular worldview or mindset, but instead, I will let my mind be transformed by God as He renews my mind (Romans 12:2).

Others may have no sense of shame living out every lustful desire they think of. I haven't learned to live that way as a disciple of Christ. He has taught me to throw off the old sinful nature of mine, which was my former way of life, and to put on my new nature which is created to be like God. The Holy Spirit will do this in me by continuing to renew my thoughts and attitudes. His desire is that I live a righteous and holy life (Ephesians 4:19-24).

I won't participate in the darkness of wild parties, drunkenness, sexual wrongdoing, immoral living, or quarreling and jealousy. Instead, I will live in the conscious awareness of the presence of the Lord Jesus Christ. I will cease to think about ways to indulge my evil desires (Romans 13:13-14).

Though I am overwhelmed by my sins, You forgive them all (Psalm 65:3).

I must die to these sinful and immoral passions and desires in me. I must deprive myself of sexual immorality, impurity, lust and sinful desires. These are like idolatry, replacing my devotion to God (Colossians 3:5).

The temptations in my life are no different from what others experience. God's faithfulness won't allow me to be tempted more than I can stand. He shows me a way out, so I can be victorious (1 Corinthians 10:13).

God shows His great love for me in that while I was the vilest sinner, Christ died for me (Romans 5:8).

I must consider myself dead to the power of sin and alive to God through Christ Jesus. I must not let sin control me and I must not give in to sinful desires. Nor should I let my body be part of sinful acts. Instead, I will give myself completely to God (Romans 6:11-13).

I will use my body as an instrument to do what is right and live holy for God's glory (Romans 6:13b).

When I confess my sins to God, He is faithful and just to forgive me of all my sins and cleanse me from all my wrongdoing (1 John 1:9).

I have discovered this principle to be true in my life—when I want to do what is right, I inevitably do what is wrong. I love God and His principles with all my heart but there is a struggle with my own appetites and desires. They wage war against my mind and make me their prisoner. I am so wretched and miserable, who will deliver me from this corrupt human existence? I am so thankful that it is Jesus Christ my Lord who will deliver me. Therefore, I am not condemned, because I belong to Him (Romans 7:21-25, 8:1).

God's will for me is that I live holy, staying away from all sexual sin. I need to control my own body and live holy with honor (1 Thessalonians 4:3-4).

If all I long for is to be rich, I am opening up myself to fall into temptations. I will end up being trapped by many foolish and destructive lusts that will plunge me into ruin and destruction (1 Timothy 6:9).

I must give honor to marriage and be faithful to my partner because God will judge those who are immoral and commit adultery (Hebrews 13:4).

I need to banish all sexual immorality, impurity, and greed from my life! This has no place in the life of a child of God (Ephesians 5:3).

I must run from sexual immorality! It affects me like no other sin. It is a sin against my body, which is a temple of the Holy Spirit given to me by God. I don't just live for my own selfish desires. I am God's child. He allowed this by paying the penalty for all my sins with the precious blood of Jesus. Therefore, I must honor and glorify God with this body He has given me (1 Corinthians 6:18-20).

I must not commit adultery (Exodus 20:14).

God instructs me to say, "No" and to turn from godless living and sinful pleasures. Instead, I should live in this evil world with self-control, wisdom, righteousness, and devotion to God (Titus 2: 12).

Christ gave His life to free me from every kind of sin. He cleanses me, making me His very own, totally committed to doing good deeds (Titus 2:14).

I don't want to be captivated by an immoral person and get involved in promiscuous sin. The Lord knows what I do and examines my actions. I don't want to end up being bound and held captive by lustful sinful addictions. Lustful actions lead to addictions and end in destruction. I will become lost because of my foolish participation (Proverbs 5:20-23).

I am acting like a fool when I commit adultery. Committing adultery will end up destroying me (Proverbs 6:32).

I must prepare my mind for action and exercise self-control. Putting all my hope in my eternity with Jesus, I must live as an obedient child of God. I can't slip back into my old ways of living selfishly, satisfying my own desires. I didn't know any better then, but now I need to be holy in everything I do, just as God, who chose me to live for Him, is holy (1 Peter 1:13-15).

Temptation

Jesus knows my weaknesses because He was tempted like me, but He did not sin. Therefore, I can receive His mercy and grace when I need it (Hebrews 4:15).

God has equipped me with all I need for doing His will. He will produce, through the power of Christ, every good thing that is pleasing to Him (Hebrews 13:21-22).

I must keep a close watch and ask God for help so that I will not give in to temptation. My spirit is willing, but alone I am weak (Matthew 26:41).

Lord, I have hidden Your Word in my heart so I won't sin against You (Psalm 119:11).

I will not conform to the secular worldview or mindset, but instead, I will let my mind be transformed by God as He renews my mind (Romans 12:2).

I am thankful that the Lord knows how to rescue godly people from their trials and temptation (2 Peter 2:9).

I must remember that God will not tempt me. That is against His character. Instead, temptation comes from inside of me, my desires that I don't squelch but, instead, let grow and drag me down. My desires, then, give way to sinful action (James 1:13-15).

I will remain sober. I will be alert and cautious at all times. Satan, the enemy of my soul, is prowling around like a roaring lion ready to pounce on me and devour me. Therefore, I will be vigilant in resisting him and constantly exercise my faith in the all-powerful true and living God who loves me (1 Peter 5:8-9).

I will be strong in the Lord and His almighty power. To stand strong against the tactics of Satan, I will put on all of God's armor. I am not fighting against ordinary enemies, but against wicked authorities, mighty powers and evil spirits in dark spiritual warfare. To win this battle, I will put on and use every piece of God's armor. This will help me resist the enemy. I will put on the belt of truth and armor, protecting my heart, which is God's righteousness. For shoes, I will wear the peace that comes from God's forgiveness. I will use the shield of faith to protect myself from the fiery arrows of the devil. I will wear the helmet of salvation and use the mighty Spirit's sword which is the Word of God (Ephesians 6:10-18).

The temptations in my life are no different from what others experience. God's faithfulness won't allow me to be tempted more than I can stand. He shows me a way out, so I can be victorious (1 Corinthians 10:13).

It is time that I realize that my body is a temple of the Holy Spirit, who lives in me and was given to me by God Himself. I don't belong to myself. I am not my own boss—I was bought by God at the highest price imaginable, the death of His Son Jesus. Therefore, I must honor God with all that I am (1 Corinthians 6:19-20).

God has called me to live a holy life, not an impure life. If I refuse to obey this, I am not disobeying manmade rules—I am ultimately rejecting God who has given me His Holy Spirit (1 Thessalonians 4:7-8).

I know that God can help me with my temptations because He has already victoriously gone through suffering and testing (Hebrews 2:18).

I know that God blesses those that patiently endure temptations and trials (James 1:12).

I want the Holy Spirit to produce His fruit in my life. The fruit is love, joy, peace, patience, kindness, goodness, faithfulness, gentleness and self-control (Galatians 5:22-23).

If all I long for is to be rich, I am opening myself to fall into temptations. I will end up being trapped by many foolish and destructive lusts that will plunge me into ruin and destruction (1 Timothy 6:9).

I belong to Christ; therefore, I will put to death my sinful passions and desires (Galatians 5:24).

Once I was full of darkness, but now I have the light of the Lord in me. So, I will live as a person of light, being careful to know what pleases the Lord and doing right. I will not participate in the worthless deeds of evil and darkness. Instead, I will expose them (Ephesians 5:8-11).

I will be careful how I live. I don't want to live like a fool—I want to live with wisdom. I will make the most of all the opportunities God has given me. I won't act thoughtlessly but will try to ascertain what the Lord wants me to do. I won't let substance take over my life because it will ruin it. Instead, I will seek to be filled with the Holy Spirit (Ephesians 5:15-18).

Christ empowers me, so I can do everything through Him using the strength He gives me (Philippians 4:13).

I cry out to God not to let me give in to temptations, instead I pray that He rescues me from the evil one (Matthew 6:13).

I admit that my Spirit is willing to stay away and not give in to temptation, but my mind and body are weak. Therefore, I will keep a lookout and pray for God's help, so I won't give into enticement (Mark 14:38).

I will pray, "Lord, forgive my sins as I forgive those that do me wrong. And please help me not to yield to temptations" (Luke 11:4).

God has called me to live a holy life, not impure. If I refuse to obey this I am not disobeying manmade rules but ultimately rejecting God who has given me His Holy Spirit (1 Thessalonians 4:7-8).

I will pray that I will not give into temptation (Luke 22:40).

When a believer I know gives in to temptation and sin then if I am mature in the Lord, I should gently and humbly help that person get back on track. I need to be careful about myself so that I do not fall into the same temptation myself (Galatians 6:1).

I must live under the control of the Holy Spirit. Then I will think about the things that are pleasing to the Spirit. Otherwise, if I allow my human sinful nature to guide me I will think and do things that are sinful (Romans 8:5).

Others may have no sense of shame living out every lustful desire they think of. I haven't learned to live that way as a disciple of Christ. He has taught me to throw off the old sinful nature of mine, which was my former way of life, and to put on my new nature which is created to be like God. The Holy Spirit will do this in me by continuing to renew my thoughts and attitudes. His desire is that I live a righteous and holy life (Ephesians 4:19-24).

God instructs me to say, "No" and to turn from godless living and sinful pleasures. Instead, I should live in this evil world with self-control, wisdom, righteousness, and devotion to God (Titus 2: 12).

Christ gave His life to free me from every kind of sin. He cleanses me, making me His very own, totally committed to doing good deeds (Titus 2:14).

I must prepare my mind for action and exercise self-control. Putting all my hope in my eternity with Jesus, I must live as an obedient child of God. I can't slip back into my old ways of living selfishly, satisfying my own desires. I didn't know any better then, but now I need to be holy in everything I do, just as God, who chose me to live for Him, is holy (1 Peter 1:13-15).

Troubles

Your presence, Lord, will go with me and give me rest (Exodus 33:14).

When my heart is distressed I can cry out to the Lord. I can pray to Him for help because he hears me. My crying reaches His ears (Psalm 18:6).

When I am desperate I can pray and the Lord will listen, He will save me from all my troubles (Psalm 34:6).

I will not be afraid or discouraged because the Lord Himself goes before me. He is with me and will never leave me or forsake me (Deuteronomy 3:18).

Even when I stumble, Your words, Lord, uphold me. You strengthen my legs and keep me from falling (Job 4:4).

When I take my troubles to the Lord and cry out to Him He hears me and answers my prayers (Psalm 120:1).

I call upon the Lord and cry out, "Lord, please save me!" He is so kind, gracious, merciful and good. He protects me when I come to Him with childlike faith (Psalm 116:4-6).

The Lord does not ignore me or belittle me when I come to Him in suffering and I am needy. He never turns His back on me. Instead, He listens to my cry for help (Psalm 22:24).

When I am distressed, I can cry out to You, Lord. Yes, I can call upon You for help. You are my God and You will hear me. My cry will reach Your ears (2 Samuel 22:7).

I lie down and sleep because You alone, Lord, make me safe (Psalm 4:8).

Lord, I rejoice in You! I am blessed. I am full of joy and singing because I take refuge in you. You protect me with Your shield of love (Psalm 5:11-12).

I love You, Lord, for You are my strength, rock, fortress, deliverer, refuge, and shield. You are the power that delivers me from my troubles. In Your presence I find safety (Psalm 18:1-2).

I am more than a conqueror through Christ who loves me. I am convinced that nothing can ever separate me from the love of God. Not death or life, angels or demons, fears about today or all my worries about tomorrow. Not even hell itself can separate me from God's love. Nothing above the sky or in the earth below, nothing in all of creation will ever, ever be able to separate me from the love of God that was given to me through Christ Jesus (Romans 8:37-39).

The Lord listens to me when I cry out to Him and gives me the discerning mind that He promised to give me (Psalm 119:169).

Even when I walk through trouble, God will preserve my life (Psalm 138:7).

I praise God, the Father of our Lord Jesus Christ, who is my merciful Father and the source of all my comfort (2 Corinthians 1:3).

Lord, You are good—a refuge in times of trouble. You care for me because I trust in You (Psalm 37:24).

I have learned how to be content with whatever I have. I know how to live with almost nothing or with everything. I have learned the secret of living in every situation, whether it is with being full or hungry, with a lot of provisions or very little. Here is the secret: I can do everything through Christ, who gives me strength (Philippians 4:11-13).

The Lord gives me power when I am weary and increases my strength when I am weak (Isaiah 40:29).

I will place myself under God's protection. I will stay with Almighty God. I will confess that God alone is my refuge, my safe place; I trust Him for He is my God (Psalm 91:1-2).

Jesus has given me a gift—a deep peace of mind and heart. This is peace the world could never give me. So, now I do not need to be troubled or afraid (John 14:27).

When I walk through a dark valley, I will choose not to be afraid. I can do this because You, O Lord, are close beside me. Like a shepherd, You protect me with your rod and staff and give me comfort (Psalm 23:4).

POWER UP!

WHEN I BELIEVE...

I am broken, no good, damaged.
I will be abandoned, banished, annihilated.
I can never be forgiven; I've gone too far.

Broken/Damaged/No Good

I have believed in Jesus and accepted him. He, therefore, gave me the privilege of becoming a child of God (John 1:12).

It is true that God's pursues me with His goodness and His unfailing love every day of my life (Psalm 23:6).

I rejoice in fully knowing that the Lord is God! He made me, and I am His. I am His, a sheep enjoying His pasture (Psalm 100:3).

When I am brokenhearted, the Lord is close to comfort me. When my spirit is crushed, He rescues me (Psalm 34:18).

God has called me by name; I am His (Isaiah 43:1).

The Lord does not ignore me or belittle me when I come to Him in suffering and I am needy. He never turns His back on me. Instead, He listens to my cry for help (Psalm 22:24).

I will forget the past and not dwell on it! Instead, I can see that God is doing a new thing (Isaiah 43:18).

I am valuable to God, so I won't be afraid. He will take care of me (Luke 12:7).

Jesus loves me as much as His Father loves Him. I believe this and focusing on His love I overflow with deep joy (John 15:9,11).

I belong to Christ and am a new person. My old life is gone and now I am living a new life (2 Corinthians 5:17).

Before God made the world, He loved me and chose me in Christ to be holy and without fault in His eyes (Ephesians 1:4).

Even though it is too great to fully understand, the life and power that comes from experiencing the love of Christ complete me (Ephesians 3:19).

I want the Holy Spirit to produce His fruit in my life. The fruit is love, joy, peace, patience, kindness, goodness, faithfulness, gentleness and self-control (Galatians 5:22-23).

For it is through God's remarkable compassion and favor, His grace, that I have been delivered from judgment and given eternal life. It was nothing I have done, it is a gift from God, so I can't take any credit for it (Ephesians 2:8-9).

I am the result of God's creation, a new masterpiece created through my relationship with Jesus Christ. He planned a long time ago that I would live for Him and do the good He has called me to do (Ephesians 2:10).

Once I was full of darkness, but now I have the light of the Lord in me. So, I will live as a person of light, being careful to know what pleases the Lord and doing right. I will not participate in the worthless deeds of evil and darkness. Instead, I will expose them (Ephesians 5:8-11).

I will be careful how I live. I don't want to live like a fool—I want to live with wisdom. I will make the most of all the opportunities God has given me. I won't act thoughtlessly but will try to ascertain what the Lord wants me to do. I won't let substance take over my life because it will ruin it. Instead, I will seek to be filled with the Holy Spirit (Ephesians 5:15-18).

Christ gave His life to free me from every kind of sin. He cleanses me, making me His very own, totally committed to doing good deeds (Titus 2:14).

The Lord gives me power when I am weary and increases my strength when I am weak (Isaiah 40:29).

I do not have to be afraid of God, for I have received God's Spirit. He has made me His child and I now affectionately call him, "Daddy, Father." God's Spirit joins with my spirit, assuring me that I am His child (Romans 8:15-16).

Heavenly Father, You have created me, You know all about my insides. You wove me together in my mother's womb. Thank You, Lord! I am full of praise because You made me so complex. Your creative powers are marvelous! How well I am aware of it! You watched me as I was being created in the darkness. You knew me before I was born! Every day of my life is recorded in Your book. You knew every moment even before I began. Your thoughts are precious toward me. I can't count them all because they are beyond numbering, more than the grains of sand. When I awake each morning, You are still with me (Psalm 139:13-18).

Abandoned/Banished/ Annihilated

I will not be afraid or discouraged because the Lord Himself goes before me. He is with me and will never leave me or forsake me (Deuteronomy 3:18).

I will be strong and courageous! I won't be afraid or full of terror. I won't panic because You, the Lord my God, will personally go ahead of me! You will not fail! You will never abandon me (Deuteronomy 31:6).

The Lord covers me with His feathers. He shelters me under His wing. I am protected, covered in the armor of His promises (Psalm 91:4).

Almighty God, You give me strength. You are my God and You save me! You are my Heavenly Father and I will praise and exalt You (Exodus 15:2).

When I am living righteously, I do not fear bad news. Instead, I have a confident trust that God will take care of me. My heart is unwavering and fearless. I can triumphantly face what comes against me (Psalm 112:6-7).

Lord God, You know me intimately. You have examined my inner being and know all about me. When I am far away from You, You still know my thoughts. You know when and where I go and when I am home. You know everything I am doing. You even know what I am going to say before I say it. You go before me and are behind me! You place Your loving hand of blessing upon me. This is all too wonderful and way more than I can comprehend (Psalm 119:1-6).

I am more than a conqueror through Christ who loves me. I am convinced that nothing can ever separate me from the love of God. Not death or life, angels or demons, fears about today or all my worries about tomorrow. Not even hell itself can separate me from God's love. Nothing above the sky or in the earth below, nothing in all of creation will ever, ever be able to separate me from the love of God that was given to me through Christ Jesus (Romans 8:37-39).

I seek for You, Lord, and Your strength. I desperately seek Your face so I can be continuously in Your presence (1 Chronicles 16:11).

The Lord does not ignore me or belittle me when I come to Him in suffering and I am needy. He never turns His back on me. Instead, He listens to my cry for help (Psalm 22:24).

Even when I stumble, Your words, Lord, uphold me. You strengthen my legs and keep me from falling (Job 4:4).

I lie down and sleep because You alone, Lord, make me safe (Psalm 4:8).

Even if I walk through the darkest valley, I will not fear, for You are right here with me. Your rod and staff comfort and protect me. You have prepared a feast for me in the presence of my enemies. You honor me, anointing my head with oil. Truly my cup overflows with blessings (Psalm 23:4-5).

Lord, I rejoice in You! I am blessed. I am full of joy and singing because I take refuge in you. You protect me with Your shield of love (Psalm 5:11-12).

I love You, Lord, for You are my strength, rock, fortress, deliverer, refuge, and shield. You are the power that delivers me from my troubles. In your presence, I find safety (Psalm 18:1-2).

I rejoice in God's unfailing love, for He sees my troubles and cares about the anguish of my soul (Psalm 31:7).

The Lord is like a father to me, tender and compassionate (Psalm 103:13).

All of God's plans for my life will work out because His faithful love endures forever (Psalm 138:8).

I trust in God and I meditate on His unfailing love for me each morning (Psalm 143:8).

I am valuable to God, so I won't be afraid. He will take care of me (Luke 12:7).

I am convinced that nothing can ever separate me from God's love (Romans 8:38).

With God's love, I have no fear because perfect love casts out all fear (1 John 4:18).

I know that God is a God of forgiveness, gracious and merciful, slow to become angry, and rich in unfailing love. He will not abandon me (Nehemiah 14:18).

Christ has given me the authority to trample on snakes and scorpions, and authority over all the power of the enemy. Nothing will harm me. God is my refuge and strength; He is always ready to help me in times of trouble. So, I will not fear (Psalm 46:1-2).

I have learned how to be content with whatever I have. I know how to live with almost nothing or with everything. I have learned the secret of living in every situation, whether it is with being full or hungry, with a lot of provisions or very little. Here is the secret: I can do everything through Christ, who gives me strength (Philippians 4:11-13).

I will be strong and take heart for I hope in the Lord (Psalm 31:24).

I do not have to be afraid of God, for I have received God's Spirit. He has made me His child and I now affectionately call him, "Daddy, Father." God's Spirit joins with my spirit, assuring me that I am His child (Romans 8:15-16).

I praise God, the Father of our Lord Jesus Christ, who is my merciful Father and the source of all my comfort (2 Corinthians 1:3).

I can say with confidence that the Lord is my helper. I will not be afraid of what man can do to me (Hebrew 13:6).

Jesus has given me a gift—a deep peace of mind and heart. This is peace the world could never give me. So, now I do not need to be troubled or afraid (John 14:27).

When I walk through a dark valley, I will choose not to be afraid. I can do this because You, O Lord, are close beside me. Like a shepherd, You protect me with your rod and staff and give me comfort (Psalm 23:4).

I am convinced that nothing can ever separate me from God's love--not death nor life, angels nor demons, fears for today nor our worries about tomorrow. Not even the powers of hell can separate me from God's love. Not power above or below the earth— indeed, nothing in all creation will ever, ever be able to separate me from the love that God has for me revealed in Christ Jesus our Lord (Romans 8:38-39).

Unforgivable/Unlovable

When I feel helpless, I'm not, because I can put my trust in You (Psalm 10:14).

God has called me by name; I am His (Isaiah 43:1).

Lord, You are good. You are my mighty refuge when trouble comes. You care for me because I put my trust in You (Nahum 1:7).

I am convinced that nothing can ever separate me from God's love (Romans 8:38).

Because Christ has made it possible for me to experience the presence of God, I am being transformed more and more like Him. This is through the working of the Holy Spirit in my life (2 Corinthians 3:18).

Lord, when I am oppressed, You are my shelter. I can run to You when I am troubled. I can trust in You for You, O Lord, will never abandon me when I search for You (Psalm 9:9-10).

The Lord does not ignore me or belittle me when I come to Him in suffering and I am needy. He never turns His back on me. Instead, He listens to my cry for help (Psalm 22:24).

Even when I am poor and needy. I am in the Lord's thoughts. He is my helper and savior. He does not delay (Psalm 40:17).

Lord Almighty, I surrender my life to You and put all my trust in You. You won't let me be put to shame. My enemies will not celebrate my defeat. Why? Because I have put my wholehearted trust in You and I will not be shamed. Only those who try to treacherously deceive others will be put to shame (Psalm 25:1-3).

When I am brokenhearted, the Lord is close to comfort me. When my spirit is crushed, He rescues me (Psalm 34:18).

When my heart is distressed, I can cry out to the Lord. I can pray to Him for help because he hears me. My crying reaches His ears (Psalm 18:6).

I rejoice in God's unfailing love, for He sees my troubles and cares about the anguish of my soul (Psalm 31:7).

All of God's plans for my life will work out because His faithful love endures forever (Psalm 138:8).

The Lord delights in me (Psalm 149:4).

Lord, when I am needy, oppressed, and have no one to help me, You will rescue me (Psalm 72:12).

With God's help, love is overflowing in my life and I am growing in knowledge and understanding (Philippians 1:9).

I have believed in Jesus and accepted him. He, therefore, gave me the privilege of becoming a child of God (John 1:12).

I am the result of God's creation, a new masterpiece created through my relationship with Jesus Christ. He planned a long time ago that I would live for Him and do the good He has called me to do (Ephesians 2:10).
Christ empowers me, so I can do everything through Him using the strength He gives me (Philippians 4:13).

Christ gave His life to free me from every kind of sin. He cleanses me, making me His very own, totally committed to doing good deeds (Titus 2:14).

I do not have to be afraid of God, for I have received God's Spirit. He has made me His child and I now affectionately call him, "Daddy, Father." God's Spirit joins with my spirit, assuring me that I am His child (Romans 8:15-16).

Acknowledgments

I was eleven years old when I started reading the scriptures. I owe that start to my Father, Jeremiah Ovitt, who challenged me to race him through the New Testament. That first reading left an indelible impression on me that has lasted my entire life.

Many thanks to the elders and teachers of Dunning Park Chapel, Jim Wallis, Don Fraser, Bob Ramey, Jim Garfield and Robert Van Slyke, who helped teach me the Word.

I want to thank my wife Janine, whose faith and trust in the Lord and reverence for the Word has been a never-ending source of inspiration for me.

For my brother Rod, who has been an example and encouragement to me to study the deeper things of the Word and has helped in the editing. Also, to Carolyn Ovitt, Rod's wife, who has been such a gift with editing, layout, and design of our materials.

I want to thank all the authors who have written the wonderful books I have read over the years that have taught me about the Word of God and how to apply it to my life. I stand on their shoulders.

Finally, I want to thank the Triune God—Father, Son, and Holy Spirit—for saving me, helping me, encouraging me, and teaching me. I pray that what has been written here will bring glory and honor to God.

MOMENT IN THE WORD
Daily Moments That Feed Your Soul

Looking for a devotional book that speaks to your deepest needs?

With a prolific career in both ministry and social causes, Ron Ovitt has provided a year-long collection of devotionals that will guide to praise, reflection, and worship. Different than most devotional books, *Moment in the Word* **speaks to everyday emotions and brings God's Word to encourage, comfort, and console.** Join the thousands of others who make Moment in the Word a part of their daily journey.

Ronald E. Ovitt, *Moment in the Word*
Gilgal Publishing, Inc.

RONALD E. OVITT BOOKS ON AMAZON

WIRED FOR MINISTRY

Activate Your Passion, Abilities, and Skills

Tired of how-to information that doesn't help you actually begin to minister?

Now there is a tool that will help you understand how you are wired for ministry! Wired for Ministry holds **the secret to activating your ministry potential by discovering your spiritual gifts, ministry preferences, ministry skills, and unique ministry drive.** This workbook culminates with the development of a Personal Ministry Profile, your unique "ministry resume." Presenting this to church or non-profit leaders will help them identify ministry opportunities that match your unique strengths and passions. Used annually at Moody Bible Institute for all incoming students, this workbook can also help you learn more about your ministry potential. Activate the ministry God has inside of you!

Ronald E. Ovitt, *Wired for Ministry*
Gilgal Publishing, Inc.

THE FIVE SIGNS OF A HEALTHY CHRISTIAN
How to Be a Spiritually Vibrant and Healthy Christian

Health is on everyone's mind. Are you a *healthy* Christian?

Our personal health, the health of our nation, the health of our economy—all with good reason. When things are unhealthy, bad things start to happen. But what about the health of our Christian experience? The Five Signs of a Healthy Christian will lead you to investigate your own spiritual health and encourage you to make adjustments where necessary. There are five signs that are general indicators that we are spiritually alive. **If you keep focused on these factors, praying over them and taking baby steps toward improving where needed, you will find yourself living a healthy Christian life!** This workbook will help motivate and encourage you in maintaining a deep and meaningful spiritual life.

Ronald E. Ovitt, *The Five Signs of a Healthy Christian*
Gilgal Publishing, Inc.

GILGAL
PUBLISHING

Available at
amazon

Made in the USA
Middletown, DE
02 October 2018